50

THE TROUBLE WITH DILBERT

PRESIDENT DILBERT

How Corporate Culture Gets the Last Laugh

OTHER BOOKS BY NORMAN SOLOMON

Wizards of Media Oz:
Behind the Curtain of Mainstream News
(co-authored with Jeff Cohen)
1997

Through the Media Looking Glass:
Decoding Bias and Blather in the News
(co-authored with Jeff Cohen)
1995

False Hope: The Politics of Illusion in the Clinton Era
1994

Adventures in Medialand:
Behind the News, Beyond the Pundits
(co-authored with Jeff Cohen)
1993

The Power of Babble:
The Politician's Dictionary of Buzzwords and Doubletalk
for Every Occasion
1992

Unreliable Sources:
A Guide to Detecting Bias in News Media
(co-authored with Martin A. Lee)
1990

Killing Our Own:
The Disaster of America's Experience With Atomic Radiation
(co-authored with Harvey Wasserman)
1982

THE TROUBLE WITH DILBERT

How Corporate Culture Gets the Last Laugh

Norman Solomon

Common Courage Press   Monroe, Maine

Cover by Matt Wuerker

Library of Congress Cataloging-in-Publication Data
Solomon, Norman, 1951-
The trouble with Dilbert:
how corporate culture gets the last laugh/ Norman Solomon
p. cm
Includes index.
ISBN 1-56751-133-3 (lib. bdg.). -- ISBN 1-56751-132-5 (pbk)
1. Adams, Scott, 1957- Dilbert. 2. Comic books, strips, etc.--
United States--History and criticism. 3. Corporate culture--United
States. 4. Industrial relations--United States. 5. Industrial manage-
ment--Social aspects--United States. I. Title.
HD58.7.S65 1997
741.5'973--DC21   97-30118
CIP

Common Courage Press
Box 702
Monroe, ME 04951

207-525-0900   fax: 207-525-3068

Second Printing

Contents

Foreword

by Tom Tomorrow

*DILBERT'S CREATOR.

CHAPTER 1

THE IMPORTANCE OF BEING DILBERT

When Scott Adams of *Dilbert* fame takes up his pen, he strikes a blow for overworked, underpaid and badly managed employees.

—*U.S. News & World Report*, April 22, 1996

"Actually," Adams laughed, "my only intention is for people to transfer their money to me."

—*Editor & Publisher*, April 19, 1997

Nobody can doubt that *Dilbert* is a smash hit—a genuine national phenomenon—a beloved icon for millions of downtrodden office workers. In a typical testimonial, *Inc.* magazine declared that *Dilbert* "has given voice to people all over America who have just about had it with management fads and corporate jargon."

Meanwhile, *People* magazine proclaimed: "While Corporate America chants its mantra of downsizing, Dilbert, cartoonist Scott Adams' tuber-shaped alter ego, appears to be subversively upsizing. His puzzled visage appears on office walls from coast to coast, pinned there by disgruntled employees who have made Dilbert their '90s-style symbol of passive resistance."

But there's a problem: Far from being subversive or promoting resistance (passive or otherwise), *Dilbert* is a fraud.

It turns out that the man behind the cartoon has little solidarity for the multitudes of *Dilbert* fans. His support for those who toil in corporate cubicles is more superficial than real.

Dilbert's creator doesn't object to downsizing. In fact, he's in favor of firing a lot of employees to boost profits.

In 1996, a *Newsweek* cover story on *Dilbert* included this cryptic sentence: "Surprisingly, Scott Adams himself thinks that downsizing does make the workplace more efficient—fewer workers means less time to waste on idiotic pursuits like vision statements, meetings and reorganizations."

I asked Adams for clarification.

"I'm not sure how to make that clearer," he replied. "When there are lots of people, they tend to spend all their time doing things that interfere with other people, e.g., setting standards, creating processes, writing vision statements, reorganizing."

He added: "In contrast, small companies don't even consider such things because they don't have the luxury to do anything but important things. I personally experienced a huge decrease in bureaucracy at Pacific Bell that seemed mostly related to the downsizing. It's obviously not an absolute statement, but it's certainly true for many of the white-collar groups in previously bloated companies."

That's it—the complete and unedited explanation from Scott Adams, hero of long-suffering office workers.

Now we know. Pink slips are good because they allow people who don't get them to experience "a huge decrease in bureaucracy."

Dilbert is an attack on middle management. Adams avoids taking aim at the highest rungs of corporate ladders—where CEOs and owners carry on... unseen and unscathed.

—*The Dilbert Principle*, p. 156

Publicists for the bestselling *Dilbert* books claim that Adams is "ripping aside the flimsy corporate curtain," and media coverage often echoes such hype. A front-page spread in *USA Today* explained that Scott Adams "has tapped a deep vein of disenchantment with the workplace."

There's no doubt that in this era of stagnant wages, the disenchantment is real—and justified. But it's worth pondering that many in top management view Adams as an ally.

Dilbert is a "cult hero to millions of American workers" at the same time that "CEOs hang him on the wall," *Business Week* has reported. "Executives say Dilbert provides an escape valve—even for the targets of his criticism." The magazine's headline summed it up:

"CORPORATE AMERICA'S PET GADFLY: Comic-strip cutup Dilbert is a hit with the execs he lampoons."

In the spring of 1995, the daily bible of corporate America—the *Wall Street Journal*—played a pivotal role in Adams' career by printing his essay titled "The Dilbert Principle." As Adams later noted in his book of the same name, "It got a huge response and led to the creation of this book."

With some fanfare in May 1997, the *Dilbert* strip began to appear in the *Wall Street Journal* as a weekly ad for a big software firm eager to link its corporate fortunes with *Dilbert*. "Our sponsorship of the *Dilbert* comic adds value to our overall strategic objectives," said Marc Sokol, senior vice president of Computer Associates International. "We are pleased to present this popular workplace icon to *Wall Street Journal* readers. Working with *Dilbert* underscores our own business philosophy and adds a unique dimension to our corporate advertising."

More and more, *Dilbert* has become schizoid by design—both a cherished mascot of oppressed workers and a valued marketing tool for companies oppressing them. The comic strip's namesake may have no mouth, but he has seemed real enough for *People* magazine to name Dilbert as one of "the twenty-five most intriguing people" of 1996—right up there with Bob Dole, Tiger Woods, Dennis Rodman and Madonna. In 1997, *Time* put Dilbert on the cover as one of the twenty-five "Most Influential People in America."

Says the cover flap of *The Dilbert Principle*: "Millions of office dwellers tack Scott Adams' comic strip to their walls when murdering the boss is not an acceptable option." (Other options, such as union organizing or public protest, go unmentioned.) *Dilbert* is a humorous safety valve, threatening to only the most rigid supervisors. As a friend commented recently, "Even my jerk of a boss likes *Dilbert*."

Across the United States, and in dozens of other countries, a gamut of *Dilbert* paraphernalia now provides the trappings of faux rebellion.

The comic's main characters never stop acting out the equivalent of corporate gallows humor. And after bouncing off the cubicle walls for so long, their bruises have festered into chronic self-loathing.

> "If you can come to peace with the fact that you're surrounded by idiots, you'll realize that resistance is futile, your tension will dissipate, and you can sit back and have a good laugh at the expense of others."
>
> —Scott Adams, *The Dilbert Principle*, p. 7

Dilbert marketers keep promoting "the comic strip for anyone surrounded by idiots"—a concept that Adams has eagerly pushed. But if, as he never tires of asserting, "we're all idiots," then we can't really expect much from ourselves or each other. Like old battery acid, the spillover of contempt becomes corrosive.

In his introduction to *The Dilbert Principle*, Adams tells readers: "I don't underestimate your intelligence. I mean, how could I?"

Maybe we've overestimated *Dilbert*.

———————⊰•⊱———————

Dilbert is clever and witty at times. It speaks to some real problems and concerns. Many people appreciate its caustic relevance to their everyday work lives.

Most readers assume that *Dilbert*—and Scott Adams—is laughing with them. But is he actually laughing *at* them?

To crack the *Dilbert* code is to decipher how *Dilbert*—and much else in mass media—can expose easy truths and avoid tougher ones at the same time.

Dilbert is a contrived rorschach—a cultural product ambiguous enough to simultaneously delight the CEO and the office worker. Scott Adams has come up with a well-designed ink blob, endearing to the corporate elite as well as to many of those who despise that elite. In the space of a few weeks, during the winter of 1996-97, Dilbert was on the cover of *Fortune*, *Newsweek* and *TV Guide*.

A lot of fans believe that *Dilbert* conveys a strong anti-corporate message. For that matter, even many commercials on television could be seen as "anti-establishment." But corporate America is not selling us the rope to hang it with; corporate America is selling us the illusions to exculpate it with. To mistake pop-culture naughtiness for opposition to the corporate system is an exercise in projection—and delusion.

It would be an understatement to say that Scott Adams and various corporate partners have astutely marketed the *Dilbert* rorschach. They bank on crucial realities—including eroded cultural sensibilities and corporatized public discourse. (Things have been deteriorating so badly that any day now Ronald McDonald will be touted in certain precincts as a countercultural figure.) Created by a cartoonist with an M.B.A., *Dilbert* brilliantly melds irreverence and sycophancy in a corporate crucible.

Many other media icons have long burbled around in the same cauldron. Consider ABC's Ted Koppel. In June 1986, *Newsweek* observed the major gap between Koppel's image and function: "The anchor who makes viewers feel that he is challenging the powers that be on their behalf is in fact the quintessential establishment journalist." (The magazine meant no offense.)

For his part, Koppel has publicly ruminated about similarities between watching *Wheel of Fortune* and *Nightline*. When he spoke at a Duke University graduation ceremony in 1987, Koppel said: "As in the case of Vanna White...many of *Nightline's* viewers project onto me those opinions that they would like me to hold, and then find me compatible....We have been hired, Vanna and I, to project neutrality. On television, ambiguity is a virtue."

A decade later, in mid-1997, *Dilbert's* ambiguity was central to its wide popularity as *The Dilbert Future* climbed onto the *New York Times* hardcover bestseller list and *The Dilbert Principle* ascended the *Times* softcover list.

Dilbert's highly marketable rorschach qualities are more than just the ingredients of a sales gambit. *Dilbert* flourishes in the context of mass culture that shores up the status quo by defining the tepid outer boundaries of dissent.

At best, *Dilbert* harmonizes with the muted trumpets that sound clarion calls for mild amelioration. And usually not even that. The *Dilbert* rallying cries of pseudo-rebellion are in the spirit of the advertising slogan adopted by Burger King in 1989: "Sometimes You Gotta Break the Rules." Or Toyota's proclamation, "The Line Has Been Crossed: The Revolutionary New Supra." Or cyber-hip *Wired*, the magazine of "The Digital Revolution" that calls its readers "digital revolutionaries." Corporate dominance has produced a glut of vaguely insurrectional mottos.

As downsizing evolves into a protracted rout, two out of three laid-off U.S. workers end up in lower-paying jobs. Overall, most cheerful economic news ignores a disturbing trend: The vast majority of new jobs are now in low-pay sectors of the economy. "Unemployment" may be down, but frustration is up—and so is the profusion of dead-end jobs. Angry responses from the grassroots are inevitable—and pent-up rage could go in any number of directions. From the vantage point of executive suites, the *Dilbert* direction looks pretty darn good.

———————

Once in a while, large media firms publish a book or put out a movie that is quite unfriendly to big business interests (though such occurrences have grown rarer during the 1990s). But jumbo companies are careful about directly linking their corporate logos with other symbols. That *Dilbert* is so compatible with mainline Wall Street should tell us something about a cultural product—and an era—turning anti-corporate emblems into cuddly corporate mascots with the constant ease of a Mobius strip.

According to a 1997 press release from *Dilbert* publisher HarperCollins and the Intel Corp. computer-chip giant, "Adams offers a bold, compelling vision of the society of the future, firmly grounded on the immutable principles of stupidity, selfishness, and sex—much like today, but with more advanced technology." That's where Intel comes in, eager to develop synergy with *Dilbert*.

Scott Adams launched publicity for *The Dilbert Future* by doing "virtual book signings" in stores via Intel teleconferencing technology. "I wanted a way to do book store appearances in my pajamas," the press release had Adams saying. "Intel's Video Phone technology was the perfect solution. I may never leave my house again."

The news release showcased *Dilbert* as a corporate shill: "Using Intel's Video Phone with ProShare® technology, Adams will chat with bookstore customers, who will be able to buy pre-signed copies of his latest *Dilbert* volume, *The Dilbert Future: Thriving on Stupidity in the 21st Century*."

Adams was hardly reluctant. He took the initiative, as a Northern California newspaper reported: "Adams contacted Intel to set up a series of virtual book appearances around the country. Through the technology, he could appear on big screens in the bookstores." In the book Adams was hawking he actually mocked the idea of teleconferencing, but no matter.

Like Computer Associates International, the massive Intel Corp.—fifth from the top among American companies ranked by market capitalization—found that a piece of Scott Adams™ was readily available for the right price.

But before we accuse Adams of betraying his devoted constituency of workers, we should consider the possibility that lots of *Dilbert* admirers have been more credulous than discerning.

Mesmerized with the sparkle of satire, many readers have simply assumed way too much. Which suits the *Dilbert* entrepreneur just fine. With conglomerates paying big to tie *Dilbert* to their products, Adams can continue to work both sides of a very lucrative street.

The pattern here applies to plenty of other cultural output that whizzes off assembly lines. From the network TV evening lineup to the movie stardom industry, the standard products—however unconventional on the surface—are affirmations of deeper shared faith.

If the Corporation has become the great Church of our times, the faith has truly been propagated by many subsidized apostles. Among them are large quantities of devout heathens who utter heretical little oaths while bending their knees toward the golden altars. The Church would, as the saying goes, prefer to have its heretics on the inside pissing out than on the outside pissing in. The Corporate Church cannot force obedience, but it can reward mightily.

Scott Adams attests to that. When he turned 40 in June 1997, Adams was ensconced in a "mini-mansion...that would be the envy of most of the corporate heavyweights Adams zings each day in his blockbuster comic strip," the *Fremont Argus* reported. The California newspaper quoted him as saying: "I may not be the best artist. But I'm certainly among the most commercial.... I think of myself as a businessman first and an artist second." The paper explained that by spring 1997,

Adams had "forty-three licensing agreements to distribute a variety of *Dilbert*-related merchandise from cards to toys."

For Adams, the purpose of mass culture is to make money with shrewd marketing: "Like any good business, I modified my product to make it more acceptable." The result is a point of immense pride and profits. As HarperCollins boasted in a "Dear Journalist/Producer" letter sent out in 1997: "The popularity of his strip and his previous books—*The Dilbert Principle* sold more than one million copies in hardcover—proves that Adams has mastered the art of leverage better than most hotshots in the business world."

CHAPTER 2

LAUGHING ALL THE WAY TO THE BANK

On May 25, 1997, Scott Adams appeared on Canada's national CBC Radio to promote his just-released book *The Dilbert Future*.

"Up until really the last ten years or so," he remarked, "I think it was fair to say that what was good for the company was also good for the employee. For the most part. At least you could make an argument for that. But then downsizing started, and suddenly what was good for the company was to get rid of employees. And the balance changed, and it became kind of us-against-them, and one side had all the power."

At that point, the interviewer asked: "Why did that change? What brought about that shift?"

ADAMS: "Oh, I think that when inflation was high and money was cheap and the economy was booming, that a lot of companies just loaded on the labor and ended up having jobs like 'director of creative training human resource guidance director' or something, and you had amazing amounts of jobs that weren't really terribly useful. And I would be the last one in the world who would argue that downsizing didn't do any good at all. Because in fact there was a lot of fat in a lot of organizations."

INTERVIEWER: "That sounds a little alarming. What happens if these tactics are allowed to flourish in the future?"

ADAMS: "Well, I think that the market system has a way of working itself out. Whereas right now you see that the employer seems to have all the power, because they can just downsize you if you're too much trouble and they'd like to get rid of people. But in the future— once a lot of people have decided that working for themselves is a pretty good deal and that it worked out after they left the big company—big companies are going to be begging to get these people back. And suddenly they're not going to have the option to be too unethical. They're going to have to be promising them free pony rides and everything else to get anybody to come work for a big company."

For Adams, downsizing is actually a rather upbeat topic. As he told the CBC interviewer: "When everybody you know has either been downsized or they've been threatened with it, and everybody knows somebody who came out just fine after getting downsized, suddenly it's not such a scary thing anymore, and everybody realizes that working for themselves is a pretty good deal."

Moments later, the interviewer changed the subject by saying: "I see Dilbert is now doing commercials."

Uncharacteristically, Adams paused before responding. "Uh yeah, you've seen that in Canada in particular."

"Do you not have any ethical problems with that?"

Adams laughed, a very dry (and perhaps a bit embarrassed) laugh. "Sorry, I didn't mean to actually laugh at that question."

INTERVIEWER: "Well, that's all right."

ADAMS: "It just slipped out."

INTERVIEWER: "Yeah."

ADAMS: "Uh. No, I guess I'm unique as cartoonists go in the sense that my background is business school instead of art school and you can probably see that fairly clearly in what I do with Dilbert. So I regard him as an employee and not as a, not as a piece of art."

INTERVIEWER: "Uh-huh. Right. So he doesn't have to have any principles."

ADAMS: "Needs none whatsoever."

———❧———

In a time of rampant downsizing—with notable speed-up, longer hours and increased strain for employees who remain on the job—*Dilbert* is marvelous for letting off steam from workplace pressure cookers. There's anger to burn, and not all of it can be stuffed, imploded or displaced. *Dilbert* to the rescue.

In the winter of 1996—with downsizing in the head-lines and on many workers' minds—*Newsweek* ran a story about *Dilbert* that concluded:

[M]anagers, desperate to cut costs (and reap bigger stock bonuses), are having trouble finding people to fire. They already have too few people, too demoralized, doing too much work. The solution: cut those folks' perks, benefits, even their office supplies in a manner that puts new meaning into the phrase "I gave at the office."

At least we'll have Dilbert around for counsel and comfort. If your HMO limits you to one mental-health session per annum, your vacation is downsized and your coffee break is eliminated, *Dilbert* will be one tonic you can always afford.

At least *Dilbert* is a way to vent. And vent. And vent...

In 1997, cultural critic Tom Vanderbilt wrote in *The Baffler* magazine about his experiences of working for a very large media conglomerate. During a year when the company was posting profits of nearly 20 percent, he recalled, the downsizing ax fell on a very generous co-worker who'd often helped colleagues to lighten their loads. And while the firm was buying more media outlets, "we would occasionally feel the brush of distant rumor telling us that our days, too, were numbered."

Vanderbilt added:

So what was the talk around the water cooler? Plans to organize? Formal protests over the company's shoddy personnel practices? No, no, no.

We talked about *Dilbert*. Hardly a day passed in which we made no reference to that great subverter of corporate hierarchy, in which I didn't see Dilbert's winsome visage flickering on a neighboring screen saver or peering out from a mug in the employee kitchen. In the face of real threats from a ruthless and all-too-knowing management, we turned to a fantasy office world in which managers were obvious incompetents, in which new motivational schemes were self-evidently ridiculous, and in which anonymous cubicled office drones held the real power. Even downsizing seemed innocuous in *Dilbert*, a practical joke that was always happening to someone else.

What seems remarkable about all this now is the curious relationship between *Dilbert* and all the absurd management fads and mission statements that it mocks. Its refusal to do anything more than gripe helped more to naturalize the managerial culture than to subvert it. As corporate America tears up the social contract, it should come as no surprise that *Dilbert* books have become a popular gift from managers to employees, or that executives have begun to ask the comic's author to lecture at their conferences... Symbolic acts of everyday resistance, it turns out, are healthy. They are exactly what the boss wants to see on your cubicle wall.

Dilbert does a good job of shedding satirical light on various, and sometimes vicious, absurdities in the workplace. A recurring theme is chronic malfunction. What is implicit in the comic strip—and more explicit in *The Dilbert Principle* and *The Dilbert Future*—is a yearning for the system to function well. And this sounds like common sense.

But what would be gained by more efficient operation of the gigantic contraption known as the corporate system? Streamlined, an administrative headquarters for McDonald's would still be assisting in the terminal clogging of arteries; a branch office for Bank of America would still be gouging customers with exorbitant fees on checking accounts; a Time Warner office would still be adding to the centralization of media control.

This is a time of enormous—in many cases, record—profits for corporations. But this is also a time of peril for them. Many people resent what this profitable process has been doing to their lives: layoffs, low pay, shrinking health-care benefits, heightened on-the-job tensions, overwork, heavy-handed supervision. It has become clearer that big-money investors and most workers have very divergent interests. The conflict is fundamental—whether you call it "class warfare" or not.

Dilbert does not encourage class warfare from the bottom up, except perhaps in petty and silly ways that are sure to be ineffectual. But—contrary to its reputation—*Dilbert* provides real service to the prevalent class warfare being waged from the top down.

Labor unions haven't adopted *Dilbert* characters as insignia. But corporations in droves have rushed to link themselves with *Dilbert*. Why? *Dilbert* mirrors the mass media's crocodile tears for working people—and echoes the ambient noises from Wall Street.

When April 1997 came to a close, the front page of the *New York Times* was in typical form as it heralded the latest economic news with a cheery headline—"Markets Surge as Labor Costs Stay in Check."

"The stock market rocketed yesterday to its greatest gain in more than five years," the *Times* reported. Why? Because of news that wages had barely increased. And employers hadn't shelled out more for "benefits like health insurance and pensions." The *Times* front page spotlighted the jubilant comment of a senior economist at the huge brokerage firm of Goldman, Sachs and Co.: "There is no question this is a better labor cost report than we had anticipated."

"Better" for employers. But how about working people? Well, they're not worth much ink. And they're certainly not worth hearing. The eighteen-paragraph *Times* article quoted a few current and former government economists—without a word from workers, their representatives or labor advocates.

When more money is in pay envelopes, most news reports tell us that's bad. It's "inflationary," and it means the economy is "overheating." But when stocks and bonds soar in value, that's supposed to make us all feel good about economic progress.

If stocks and bonds were equitably held by most Americans, perhaps this would be cause for cheer. Yet only 2 percent of the public owns half of the country's individual stock and bond holdings. Other people in the market are very small investors. And 80 percent of Americans have no direct stake in the stock markets at all. (Employees with indirect holdings via pension funds have no say in how the money is invested and can't get access to proceeds until they retire.)

Although most news accounts leave the impression that an upswing in the stock market augurs well for the nation's work force, the opposite has been the case. The 1990s have been a celebratory time for Wall Street—and a grim time for workers confronted with downsizing. That's no coincidence. Just as evidence of wage stagnation makes stocks rise, Wall Streeters are frequently ecstatic to learn that a major corporation has decided to slash its payroll. Downsizing usually sends stock prices climbing.

The internalized notion that what's good for the Big Corp is somehow good for us is demonstrably false. Yet it's pervasive—and made more so by the likes of *Dilbert*.

—*The Dilbert Future*, p. 125

An invisible—yet heavy—cloud of guilt pervades *Dilbert* comic strips. Between the downbeat lines are serious laments: Employees are letting the Corp down. Badly.

—*Fugitive From the Cubicle Police*, p. 217

Writing in *The Dilbert Future*, Scott Adams comes up with a broad caricature of workers as swindlers: "Employees today goof off with the telephone, e-mail, Internet connections, and their computers. It all looks like work to the unsuspecting employer."

In a similar way that news media often encourage us to identify with the fortunes of Wall Street, the *Dilbert*

—*Fugitive From the Cubicle Police*, p. 191

motif is a continuous series of riffs about how middle-management stupidity and severe employee deficiencies are depriving the Corp of its appropriate level of profits. In *Dilbert*, the Corp is the most profoundly aggrieved party—ripped off and undermined by employees who are inveterate slackers.

In *The Dilbert Future*, Adams contends: "Working for a big company was a great deal until the '90s.... Then the era of downsizing came.... [M]any of the downsizees had been avoiding real work by taking company-sponsored training courses for years.... Out of necessity, they reinvented themselves as 'self-employed' people and scrambled to create new careers that would use the skills they learned while avoiding work."

While Adams does some comic strips that may seem to frown on downsizing, he tells journalists and management seminars that he supports it. Adams relies on millions of office workers who read into his comic's calculated ambiguities what they liké while buying his books, calendars and numerous Dilbertized knick-knacks.

At the same time, the conglomerates that contract with Adams have no need to worry that *Dilbert* might raise public expectations about corporate responsibilities and human values. On the contrary, *Dilbert*—affirming "selfishness" as "immutable"—constantly lowers expectations. So does Adams' behavior in the marketplace.

"What happens with lowered expectations," Ralph Nader has observed, is that "you got to keep lowering them. That is a danger point for these conglomerates. The thing that troubles me about these executives is they have no interest in going down the abstraction ladder to see what's happening. They're dealing with numbers. They're dealing with columns. They're dealing with: are they going to get their bonus. They're dealing with their stock share."

So, in the health-care industry, "instead of calling doctors and nurses," top executives are "calling their stockbroker every day. 'How'd I do today Jack? Up three-and-a-half?' Out comes the pencil. Another million and a half bucks. This is dangerous. This is reckless. This kind of mentality is a clear and present danger to the health and safety of the American people."

A satirist might choose to find ways to skewer "this kind of mentality." But *Dilbert* does not skewer. It reinforces. Just ask the folks at the Xerox Corporation who devised something called the "Do-It-Yourself Empowerment Kit"—featuring *Dilbert*.

CHAPTER 3

A ZANY MANAGEMENT TOOL

By late 1996, *Dilbert* characters and cartoons were central to pep-talk booklets that Xerox was producing and distributing to employees.

Here's some sample language: "Why a do-it-yourself kit? Because nobody else can do it for you. And, because we believe that creating a truly Empowering Work Environment is critical to your success and to Xerox' success. We're serious. We can set the stage, clarify the concepts and provide the structure, but ultimately, creating an Empowered Work Place is something you do yourself."

Dilbert cartoon characters or complete *Dilbert* comic strips adorn nearly every page of the Xerox employee guidelines, which include formulas like "Empowerment = Growth and Productivity." In other words, the handbook explains, "Empowerment *results* in Growth and Productivity."

Like Scott Adams, the Xerox corporate voice presents the *Dilbert* office environment as something negative. And also like Adams, the Xerox handbook says that true empowerment of individuals could be measured by what good it does the corporate coffers—

"growth and productivity." (The "growth," of course, refers only to the corporation's growth.) *Dilbert* satire, Xerox declares, is beneficial "as a reminder of what empowerment *isn't.*"

What, however, *is* "empowerment"? It's something that empowers people on the Xerox payroll to shed dysfunction, gain clarity, and function more effectively to make money for the corporation. That is the *sine qua non* of *Dilbert*-as-object-lesson, the Xerox handbook emphasizes: "It's been demonstrated that an Empowering Work Environment translates directly to improved business results and increased employee satisfaction—things we all care about. There's something in this for everyone. Even the skeptics among us."

Indeed, corralling "even the skeptics among us" is a corporate task that *Dilbert* imagery is well-positioned to assist. There's little point in denying that office work is often frustrating, dumb, demeaning. But what must be blurred and denied is that top management is the worker's adversary. The cartoonish *Dilbert* symbols, secured by Xerox in this case, have been conscripted as troops in a never-ending war: to mobilize employees for the corporate quest to enlarge the profit margin.

Since Xerox workers are a highly schooled bunch, the company manual gradually escalates its equations, reaching such algebra as "Empowerment = Direction and Communication + Ownership + The Way We Work = Growth and Productivity."

"What's In It For Xerox?" a headline in the manual asks. The answer appears over a drawing of Dilbert: "Everything. A more committed, more productive work force. One that's closer to the customer and able to

implement decisions that meet customer needs and exceed customer expectations. As we said—bottom line: Improved business results."

After drawing the cartoon that later became this book's foreword, Tom Tomorrow recalls, he "caught a predictable amount of flak from apoplectic *Dilbert* fans who apparently considered this tantamount to heresy." Tomorrow "was even beginning to wonder if perhaps I had overstated my case"—until someone sent him a copy of the *Dilbert*-illustrated handbook put out for Xerox employees.

Xerox management had recognized what more gullible *Dilbert* readers did not: *Dilbert* is an offbeat sugary substance that helps the corporate medicine go down. The *Dilbert* phenomenon accepts—and perversely eggs on—many negative aspects of corporate existence as unchangeable facets of human nature ("immutable"). As Xerox managers grasped, *Dilbert* speaks to some very real work experiences while simultaneously eroding inclinations to fight for better working conditions.

"What's important here," Tom Tomorrow notes, "is that the purveyors of corporate gibberish at Xerox were not 'threatened' by *Dilbert*. Nor did they feel that the inclusion of a cartoon in which Dilbert warns a new employee to run for her life from the company's new empowerment program in any way undermined *their own empowerment program*."

Rather than presenting a hazard to corporate authority, *Dilbert* provided Xerox with help in deflecting cynicism that everyone knows exists—while supplying a kind of targeted celebrity-endorsement for Xerox managers. *Dilbert*'s make-believe office became a pedantic anti-model— "the antithesis of empowerment," the Xerox handbook explains. "Dilbert's here to get your attention. So far, it seems to be working. He's here to remind us of the behaviors and attitudes we want to avoid, and change."

Yet *Dilbert's* imprimatur on Xerox inverts any shred of subversion that readers in cubicles might have imagined. Instead of being a weapon against mind-numbing corporate blather, *Dilbert* is a tool for propagating more of it.

Not content to draft *Dilbert* characters directly into its in-house propaganda army, Xerox also opted to sprinkle Scott Adams-style prose throughout the text. (Example: "Xerox' model of the Empowering Work Environment is a conceptual model. Because it's printed on paper, technically, you could fold it up and make a paper airplane out of it, but that wouldn't make it an airplane model. Besides, we'd prefer you didn't do that.") Every page or so, some effort at whimsical wit appears, as if to say a-manager-is-just-one-of-the-guys.

Bottom line: Serving Xerox can be fun and meaningful. Seventeen pages into the handbook, at the end of Part Two, there's a drawing of Dogbert flat on his back, exclaiming: "AHHH...THE AIMLESS EMPOWERED!"

The Xerox-*Dilbert* liaison was hardly out of character for either party. In Tom Tomorrow's words, "it's just a minor artifact from a merchandizing empire gone mad. But that's not an excuse. It's one thing to be selling everything from *Dilbert* Mouse Pads to Post-It Notes to— well, to any piece of crap with a flat surface large enough to hold a legible *Dilbert*™ logo. But there's something inherently dissonant in using *Dilbert* images to illustrate exactly the sort of corporate babble Scott Adams' entire career is predicated on deconstructing."

"What's next?" Tomorrow asks. "Zany *Dilbert* termination notices, so downsized employees can enjoy a heartfelt chuckle over the hopelessness of their plight as they're being shown the door?"

The flood of *Dilbert* products can be understood as a vaccine. A mild strain of irreverence—touted as full-blown rebellion—inoculates against the authentic malady of anti-corporate fervor.

———⟫•◦•⟪———

Parallel to the fictional content of *Dilbert* is the real-life conduct of its creator. Like Michael Jordan endorsing Nike footwear and insisting that the workers making the shoes in sweatshops overseas are irrelevant to him, Scott Adams hasn't hesitated to align himself with immense corporations if they're willing to move large sums of money in his direction. Let's consider one of those firms—Intel, the world's biggest maker of computer chips.

While *Dilbert* seemed to ally itself with embattled workers, Intel's execs comprehended the shallowness of that alliance. For Intel, an arrangement with Adams was a compelling way to buff up its image.

As it happened, at the same time that Adams was endorsing Intel's Video Phone wares, the firm was blocking employees' on-the-job access to a web site put together by some dissatisfied Intel workers. The company programmed its workplace computers so that if employees tried to look at the web site, the effort would be fruitless—eliciting signals like "ABORT" or "FAIL."

Intel's management enforced the cyber-blockade without apology. After all, it abhorred the material on the web site <www.igc.apc.org/faceintel>, maintained by a group of current and former employees called "FACE Intel." A company spokesperson told the Portland-based *Willamette Week* newspaper: "In our view it's defamatory. We have a right to control how our computer system is used, and we chose not to use it for this small group of people."

This, of course, is the kind of management arrogance that Adams might lampoon in *Dilbert*. But the contradictions go much deeper. As the blockaded web site spells out in grim detail, Intel is in the midst of making war on its work force—with managers ordered to continue a downsizing process by implementing "termination quotas." The ratcheted-up pressures on Intel employees have caused extreme and protracted stress for many. The FACE Intel group says it wants to inform the public "about how far Intel goes in the quest of higher profits and productivity, without regard to human needs or capabilities."

While posting profits of $5.2 billion in 1996, Intel persisted with its push to eliminate jobs. "Managers are forced to target the most vulnerable from those that are left," FACE Intel explains. "These competent, contributing individuals are unfortunately targeted for termination. Managers justify this corruption by attempting to build a case of inadequacy against the targeted employee. These cases are unfounded and unreasonable. Some of those targeted are employees who are too 'expensive,' compared to the replacement employee, a new college graduate."

At age 53, former Intel engineer Ken Hamidi ruefully remembered how he sometimes put in workdays that lasted eighteen or twenty hours. "They have you working 150 percent of capacity," he said. In the long run, many suffer: "A lot of people are seeing psychologists, having nervous breakdowns, heart attacks, suicides. It's the number one company in the world, but it's a miserable place to work." According to the sample survey done by FACE Intel, "over 90 percent of the employees targeted for termination are over the age of 40."

Perhaps it's no accident that Scott Adams displays special contempt for people who have been around for several decades. In *The Dilbert Future*, old people are targets of particular derision. Adams sees scant value in the elderly; as producers they're close to worthless and as consumers they're basically in the way, moving slowly and holding up progress in checkout lines. He writes that "the only thing worse than being surrounded by Induhviduals is being surrounded by senior citizen Induhviduals."

On May 22, 1996—a year before *Dilbert* became another marketing accessory for Intel Corp.—the company's chief operating officer, Craig Barrett, told the Intel stockholders meeting: "The half-life of an engineer...is only a few years."

Dilbert humor is sublimely safe for Intel, and Xerox ($26 billion in assets), and the other conglomerates embracing it—precisely because the *Dilbert* boundaries are so reliable. The running gags stay inside the moat of the corporate castle. Scott Adams is an impish yet loyal subject, a court jester who has proven his eagerness to serve the royal highness in a land where cash is king.

The contrast with the creator of *Calvin and Hobbes* is striking. Bill Watterson rebuffed all attempts to create spinoff products featuring the little boy Calvin and his come-alive stuffed tiger. In plush suites where multi-million-dollar tie-ins are automatic, Watterson's stubborn sense of integrity was exceptional.

Zeal to squeeze every drop of commerce out of *Dilbert* is consistent with the temper of Adams' cartoons and books: The corporate contest is the only game worth playing, and the glorious option is for the few winners to run up the dollar score as high as they can. The many losers try to cope as best they can.

All this is in sync with the mass-media scenery and hardly seems conspicuous. On the contrary, the ideology that enthralls Adams blends with the dominant messages from mass media every day—so ubiquitous that they're taken for granted as part of the natural terrain.

Institutional labyrinths keep promoting "a view of the world which controls perceptions of what is, and limits the possibilities of what might be," wrote political scientist Paul N. Goldstene. We continuously meet power "concentrated and screened from perception which it increasingly constructs"; we are moving to "a condition where the effects of power are pervasive, but where its identity is lost."

So *Dilbert*, like much other mass-marketed culture, adds to the despair that it evokes. The result is not so much laughter as sighs of recognition and further resignation. *Dilbert* is among a wide range of products acclaimed for their high jumps over low standards.

Like news media, mass-culture products routinely guide Americans away from awareness of how, and for what purposes, they're shaped by corporate forces so widespread as to be almost anonymous. We are guaranteed to have plenty of company in a disorienting—and numbing—process.

While language, art, dialogue and debate are valuable tools for digging out of messy quandaries, words have been looted of meaning. After the thousands of times we've heard the word "freedom" used in political speeches and TV commercials, for instance, how readily can we invoke or feel its meaning? The Xerox-*Dilbert* employee handbook, by the way, promises that workers will gain "freedom" by following its cues.

A never-ending din of white noise equates the mouthing of a word with what it's supposed to represent. The image associated with a timeworn word commonly precedes, and preempts, thought. As Stuart Chase noted a half-century ago, "Identification of word with thing is well illustrated in the child's remark 'Pigs are rightly named, since they are such dirty animals.'" Words supplant meaning, with verbiage its surrogate and clichés its frequent enemy. Thus are the arsenals of confusion stockpiled and fired, laying siege to our own futures—until, as Jimi Hendrix anticipated, "the life that led us is dead."

All we ever have is daily life. When so much of it is taken up with doing things we don't particularly want to do, going through motions of being who we don't particularly want to be, our lives are slipping away. As one uneasy hectic day follows another, many workers yearn for a substantive remedy. *Dilbert* is a cynical placebo.

Praise for Adams reached a fever pitch with *The Dilbert Principle*'s zooming sales in 1996. *Newsweek* proclaimed that "the contrast between *Dilbert* and real life is...almost nonexistent." *Time* asserted: "Every calamity has its bard, and downsizing's is Scott Adams." *Business Week* dubbed the top-selling book "part comic collection, part management-book parody, and all antiboss."

Dilbert may be "antiboss." But so is *Blondie*.

For decades, Dagwood's perennial enemy has been Mr. Dithers, a boss with techniques of oppression ranging from the guilt trip and the blatant threat to out-and-out physical assault. But to read *Blondie*—or *Dilbert*—is hardly to partake of an anti-corporate polemic. Among their many functions, middle managers serve as flak-catchers in lieu of those with appreciably more power in the Organization.

—*Fugitive From the Cubicle Police*, p. 183

To vilify Mr. Dithers—or the fellow with the devilish pair of tufts on his head who afflicts Dilbert, Wally and Alice—is to engage in a timeless shtick. Yes, Scott Adams' humor is more "sophisticated"—it's layered with countless references to maddening techno-babble and fatuous management cant—but it remains in a pandering groove. Let's take Adams at his word: "Like any good business, I modified my product to make it more acceptable."

Dilbert has no major quarrel with the biggest bosses of all. While no doubt many Microsoft employees tack *Dilbert* strips to their bulletin boards, why would Bill Gates mind? *Dilbert* is no more likely to inspire an insurrection against his awesome power than the president's next State of the Union address.

In *The Dilbert Future*, Scott Adams writes with admiration, even reverence, about Gates. ("How smart is he really? Smart enough not to let you know how smart he is.") When a cartoon has Dogbert saying that he's writing an article to "explain why I'm smarter than the entire Microsoft Corporation," Dilbert bristles and retorts: "Actually, they're mostly geniuses. And many are millionaires." That's about as close as *Dilbert* ever gets to unabashed idealism.

"It's difficult to think of a company in the history of the world that's positioned to influence so many aspects of life as Microsoft is at the end of the 20th century," Silicon Valley investor Michael Moritz commented in late 1996. "In terms of a civilized world, you'd have to go back to the Roman Empire to find any organization that had as great a reach as Microsoft has today."

Dilbert's criticism of the Corporate Church is so diluted that it's now sprinkled like holy water as a Church ritual.

———❖———

"In an age of advanced technology," Aldous Huxley foresaw in his introduction to *Brave New World*, "inefficiency is the sin against the Holy Ghost." The vice, the depravity against which the *Dilbert* strip and its creator constantly inveigh is the sinful absence of efficiency.

Implicit in many of the *Dilbert* comics, and in the writings of Scott Adams, is the assumption that efficiency should reign supreme. Efficiency Almighty. Bypassing this kingdom of goodness is idiotic—but more importantly, it is blasphemous.

To hear Adams spin his endless tale, the great sin of bureaucracies—and the "idiots" within them—is chronic inefficiency. Failure to come anywhere near the lofty ideal is frequent grist for the *Dilbert* mill. The credo of a worthy office worker—I am efficient, therefore I am—cannot be stated with honesty by anyone in Dilbertland.*

It may seem surprising or counterintuitive—but in the corporate jihad of the mid-1990s, *Dilbert* became a stealth weapon against workers. After all, bosses cracking whips commonly have about as much credibility as a slavemaster threatening galley slaves. But a clever satire of inefficiency can go where no whip-cracking is able to penetrate.

Top-echelon corporate managers have good reason to smile on a popular cartoon that hammers away at some of their favorite messages aimed at workers: Inefficiency is really idiotic. Don't you yearn for efficiency? Isn't the lack of it the root of our problems here?

⟶•◄

A lot of what's in mass media doesn't seem to have anything to do with our daily routines. But *Dilbert* affirms some firsthand experiences. The comic strip—fanciful yet

---

*While *Dilbert's* plodding office is a den of slothful iniquity, the '90s mythos has portrayed wondrous spaces where upper-crust managers soar. "Next time you're watching a football game on TV," suggests *The Baffler's* editor-in-chief Thomas Frank, "count the number of commercials that star the noble businessman, striding in slow motion across the tarmac at sunset; standing with arms akimbo atop his skyscraper and surveying his domain; relaxing in business class as the thoughtful stewardess gently sees to his needs...performing miracles of pie-chart transmission or conference-calling from some improbable place (golf course, igloo)."

weirdly realistic—seems to be "on our side" against the petty gauntlets of nonsense in the workplace.

Most people have very little control over their job. Employees are afraid to be open about perceptions that might not sit well with supervisors. At work we're supposed to strive to be smart—but not too smart. In fact, taking a mental dive often seems wise. A motto might be: Dummy up for safety.

Dilbert satirizes and reinforces the dumbness of the workplace. The comic says that middle-management emperors have no clothes—but the *Dilbert* material is part of the pop-culture fabric shielding the empire from scrutiny.

Many managers are happy to get on a *Dilbert* bandwagon that isn't going much of anywhere. *Dilbert* tells a daily cautionary tale that most bosses can acknowledge some truth in: Many workplaces are stifling. Alienated employees are less happy and, in the long run, less productive. Etc. And bottlenecked communication impedes feedback for creative solutions.

While workers are often frustrated and angry, it's hazardous to express such emotions directly. And yet the frustration and anger are clear realities. As the management of Xerox came to see, *Dilbert* can help to define very real problems in narrow terms.

Technical expertise is on a pedestal—great precision is sought in dealing with computers, for instance—but fuzziness customarily prevails with reference to power. Whatever is understood privately, little is discussed openly about dynamics of leverage and manipulation. *Dilbert* cuts only at the margins, dissecting management's techniques but not its basic prerogatives. *Dilbert* challenges corporate dysfunction but not corporate function.

To speak bluntly about power inequities—and to work with others to challenge them—could be truly threatening to corporate poohbahs. In contrast, sarcasm is fine. *Dilbert* does not suggest that we do much other than roll our eyes, find a suitably acid quip, and continue to smolder while avoiding deeper questions about corporate power in our society.

Huge fortunes keep being made on the fairly safe bet that we will remain anesthetized. *Dilbert* adjusts—and fortifies—the terms of the numbing, to take into account the undeniable alienation that besets so many workplaces.

Dilbert's mockery of office workers, couched in pretenses of universality, insists that stupidity and selfishness are central to who we are—and must be. So, readers are encouraged to believe, there's little need to explore how we ought to be relating to each other in more ideal circumstances that can never really exist.

Dilbert cartoons calcify the essence of the repressive workplace. *Dilbert* books expound on how that workplace could become a lot more efficient and maybe a bit less distasteful. Humane values aren't on the agenda. Why would we expect they might be?

"Historically," Ralph Nader has pointed out, "you control people by lowering their expectations." This is true in the workplace and other spheres of life. The diminishing of what we could or should expect—from ourselves, and each other, and institutions—normalizes what we find unpleasant or worse. For corporate elites, that diminishment is a pleasure to behold. In Nader's words: "If our expectations are low, they have control."

42

Things You'll Always See in *Dilbert*:

* Stupid bosses
* Stupid management practices and buzzwords
* Stupid co-workers
* Stupid people in other departments
* Stupid temps, interns, and consultants
* Stupid technological innovations

Real Problems Which—to Its Credit— *Dilbert* Acknowledges:

* Outsourcing of labor to temporary help
* Staff restructuring as a result of downsizing and corporate takeovers
* Expanded workdays
* Minimizing of employees' physical space

Major Issues

That *Dilbert* Rarely or Never Addresses,

Although It Certainly Could:

* Export of jobs to cheap labor markets
* Outsourcing to prison labor
* Outsourcing to workfare labor
* Workplace racism
* Union-busting
* Corporate welfare
* Repetitive stress injuries, exposure to chemicals, and other work-related hazards
* Urine testing, polygraph examinations, and other invasive corporate security measures
* Sexual harassment
* The glass ceiling for women
* Planned obsolescence
* The export to Third World markets of products too hazardous to sell in the United States
* Cost-benefit analysis defining a finite number of work-place injuries or deaths as acceptable
* Pension fund fraud
* Tax abatements and subsidies for unnecessary projects
* Golden parachutes for CEOs, early retirement for employees
* Hiring of lobbyists and "soft money" donations to bribe politicians into passing favorable legislation
* "Deregulation"-driven elimination of safety codes, health laws, and barriers to monopoly
* The Federal Reserve's manipulation of interest rates and the money supply to maintain a fixed percentage of unemployed and underemployed people, thereby ensuring workplace insecurity

Two Other Things
You Don't See Much of in *Dilbert:*

* CEOs, shareholders, board members, and the other owners of capital who actually have power
* Blue-collar workers who actually make the stuff that Dilbert designs—people who, incidentally, face many of the same problems he does, and with far less ability to do anything about it

— Bob Harris

(For more commentary from Bob Harris, see Chapter 5—"A Humorist's View of *Dilbert*.")

CHAPTER 4

"IT'S JUST A CARTOON..."

There are many ways to defend *Dilbert*:
- It's clever.
- It's funny.
- It's just a cartoon.
- It's a witty spoof of daily life at the office.
- It uses humor to make people feel better about work-place predicaments.
- It's a force for workplace sanity.
- It lowers blood pressure.
- It exposes the management stupidities and absurdities that millions of people face at work.
- It shouldn't be taken too seriously.
- And anyway, different people read it different ways.

——⇒•⇐——

It's true that *Dilbert* is sometimes clever. And funny.

And the essays by Scott Adams include some imaginative writing.

Yet cleverness and imagination are not abstract qualities. They're tied to content...attitude...and values.

These days, *Dilbert* is hardly "just a cartoon." By 1997, United Feature Syndicate was calling it the most widely distributed comic strip in the United States. And *Dilbert's* reach is global; the syndicate claims that it appears in 1,700 newspapers worldwide, in seventeen languages and fifty-one countries. The publisher of *The Dilbert Future* says that every day "*Dilbert* is currently read by more than 150 million readers."

Dilbertization has just begun. With *Dilbert* hardcovers in the million-seller range, plenty more are on the horizon; in early 1997, *Entertainment Weekly* magazine reported that "HarperBusiness will publish four more hardcover books in the next five years, and Andrews & McMeel hopes to roll out calendars and softcover collections of strips for the next seven." Meanwhile, across the planet, *Dilbert* cartoons are appearing on calendars, coffee mugs, cards, clothes and scads of other products.

Perhaps most significantly in the long run, *Dilbert* has become a mass-marketed attitude—a public way of coping—while we encounter the tightening vise of corporatization. The *Dilbert* phenomenon is part of a process making people more accustomed to a stance of ironic passivity.

To say that the proliferation of *Dilbert* lacks social importance or impact is to claim that mass culture doesn't matter much—that it doesn't affect how we perceive or act on our perceptions—that it doesn't influence how we talk and think and live. In fact, how we use words is a marker and pointer for our outlooks. As George Orwell observed, everyday language "becomes ugly and inaccurate because our thoughts are foolish, but the slovenliness of our language makes it easier for us to have foolish thoughts."

Certainly no advertising exec can afford to underrate the consequences of words, images and marketed attitudes. The ad industry deals in hard numbers and

empirical results. Billions of dollars get spent every season in the USA on the well-tested assumption that what keeps flashing before our eyes and ears has major effects on what we buy. And buy into.

Mega-marketing requires, more than ever, a capital-intensive blitz. To saturate the grassroots, mass-mediated "popular culture" needs a nod from a big-money suite somewhere. In the nationwide amphitheater, would-be creators are to remain in their seats unless summoned to the stage by someone with appreciable monetary clout. The audience does not create. The audience consumes.

As Thomas Frank puts it: "No longer can any serious executive regard TV, movies, magazines, and radio as simple 'entertainment,' as frivolous leisure-time fun: writing, music, and art are no longer conceivable as free expressions arising from the daily experience of a people. These are the economic dynamos of the new age, the economically crucial tools by which the public is informed of the latest offerings, enchanted by packaged bliss, instructed in the arcane pleasures of the new, taught to be good citizens, and brought warmly into the consuming fold."

＞＞●＜＜

So what is *Dilbert* selling, along with comics, books and other Dilberphernalia? When we buy it—literally and psychologically—what are we accepting?

To praise *Dilbert* as an uplifting or positive force is to ignore the contexts of present-day corporate theology. The sight of CEOs and office workers singing from the same *Dilbert* hymnal should give us pause, especially as

Scott Adams essays increasingly claim to explain the meaning of modern work and the proper options ahead for corporate management.

The spring 1997 issue of *Office Depot Business News* reported that the *Dilbert* comic strip "caught the imagination of millions of white-collar workers fed up with 'downsizing,' 'rightsizing,' 're-engineering' and other examples of corporate ineptitude masquerading as efficient management."

Unfortunately, the "imagination" that *Dilbert* caught was already problematic. To the extent that we accept the limits of mass-marketed imagination, they become our own. And no major changes for the better can come about unless we break through the limitations that often go unrecognized because they've become so familiar.

Adams conveys no interest in solidarity between men and women, or between people of different races. Sexism and racism seem to bother him not at all. In *The Dilbert Future*, he lists "mandatory sexual harassment training" and "mandatory diversity training" among half a dozen "Productivity-Thwarting Activities."

In *Dilbert* comics, feminists assert themselves by doing things like wielding a crossbow or physically pounding men. In a 1994 episode, Dilbert's date sits at the restaurant table and tells him: "I'm a '90s kind of woman. I demand equality but the man must pay for dinner. And recent surveys show that many women my age think it's okay to slap a man."

Believing that *Dilbert* provides incisive satire about our situations as human beings in the late 1990s is an exercise in devotion. As a set of satiric theses nailed to the Corporate Church door, *Dilbert* cartoons and books retain the essential faith. It is a belief based on a truncated sense of possibilities for the creation of popular art that could resonate deeply and profoundly, in personal and social terms.

Cute little jokes, mass produced, can dominate a sparse field of corporatized dreams. Funny and meaningful. But compared to what?

Okay, *Dilbert* is irreverent—compared to most comic strips in daily papers, which have little to say and keep saying it. Irreverent in *style*, *Dilbert* is substantively reverent toward the essential elements of corporate domination. Amid all his wisecracks, Adams quibbles about how to revise that domination.

Throwing stark light on unpleasant absurdities without the slightest hope of solutions for the common good, Scott Adams digs the readers into a deepening trough. In his estimation, the only way out is an individual escape—a point that Adams has emphasized since leaving his mid-level phone company job in 1995.

———⟫•⟪———

"The gutsiest professionals are already quitting their jobs and going it alone," Adams gloats in *The Dilbert Future*, "but they're the exception. Most professionals are like sheep." On another page he declares: "I'm convinced that my job situation is a model of the future."

Adams appears to be sharing his insights—combining his humor with helpful tips for the average reader. In this way, *Dilbert* books may indeed seem to be aiding workplace sanity, suggesting better alternatives for office employees who feel trapped.

But few people will strike it rich on their own—in cartooning or any other venture—and most will find the go-it-alone dream to be as disappointing as a mirage. For each successful entrepreneur, many more fail. Meanwhile, the vast majority of distressed workers will do their best to hang onto their cubicle jobs in the first place—not, as Adams implies, because of a shortage of brains or zest for life, but rather because that's how the system is structured.

The sharp *Dilbert* tone that routinely slices into middle management—and grows duller on the rare occasions that it swipes at corporate higher-ups—is a double-edged blade that cuts deeply against the rank-and-file office worker. And against the lowly human being in general. The *Dilbert* tenor is often contemptuous of garden variety people—mockingly dubbed "Induhviduals" in *The Dilbert Future*.

Ha ha. Get it? Most people are so dense that "duh" may as well be their middle names. Adams confers special dispensation on those who read *Dilbert* books, of course; their wisdom is attained by willingness to fork over money in his direction. As a clever marketer, Adams recognizes that the paying customers must be kept out of his nonstop line of fire.

> "There are two types of people in the world: the bright and attractive people like yourself who read *Dilbert* books, and the 6 billion idiots who get in our way. Since we're outnumbered, it's a good idea not to refer to them as idiots to their faces."
>
> —Scott Adams, *The Dilbert Future*, p. 1

Even so, Adams doesn't always restrain his sweeping contempt. (Only a few pages of *The Dilbert Principle* go by before his notification to readers, "I don't underestimate your intelligence. I mean, how could I?") At every moment, the venom threatens to splatter on those who are savoring the spectacle of it falling elsewhere.

Despite his image as a breaker of conventional molds, Adams operates in the dispiriting spirit of most TV comedy. Media critic Mark Crispin Miller's apt description of televised humor applies to *Dilbert*: it offers "not a welcome but an ultimatum—that we had better see the joke or else turn into it."

Adams' ridicule of "Induhviduals" may be enjoyable for those who feel out of range of his nasty spit. *Dilbert* invites us to appreciate that *finally* a successful cartoonist/author is showing just how contemptible some people really are. His depictions of the obnoxious and the asinine plainly apply to the jerks who try our patience and waste our precious time because they're so dumb—and, even worse, because they're our co-workers or even our supervisors. Later it might dawn on us that we fall within his big circle of disdain.

CHAPTER 5

A HUMORIST'S VIEW OF *DILBERT*

Bob Harris—like Dilbert—earned his degree in electrical engineering and began his career working in a cubicle for a giant corporation.

But Harris quit his job after several months. These days, he's a full-time satirist. He has performed at hundreds of comedy clubs and colleges. In 1997, his daily commentaries were airing on the radio in Los Angeles, and his column "The Scoop" was appearing in alternative newsweeklies.

I asked Harris to assess the *Dilbert* phenomenon, and he came back with a detailed response. "It started out short," his cover note said, "but the more I researched the angrier I got."

So, Bob Harris wrote the rest of this chapter:

Real-life Dilberts hang episodes of the comic strip on their cubicle walls the way prisoners decorate their cells with letters from home. Favorite panels are xeroxed and circulated like samizdat leaflets behind the iron curtain.

Dilbert is a rising star in the board room as well. What began as a sweet-natured strip about the life of a hapless drone has evolved into what appears to be a bracing critique of incompetent management. Adams is a hot speaker at conferences of Fortune 500 companies, his line of business training videos is popular, and his books on management are all bestsellers.

Obviously, there's a major social trend here.

What we laugh at tells us a lot about ourselves. Laughter is an involuntary response, one that doesn't occur easily if you're uncomfortable. Which means it's a lot easier to get laughs by confirming existing perceptions than by challenging them.

Compare the stand-up careers of Bill Hicks and Andrew Dice Clay. Both were perceived as late 1980s "outlaws" (whatever that means when you're headlining a franchised comedy club and helping to sell corporate beer and snack foods to a bunch of bloated yuppies). Both favored controversial subject matter. Both were occasionally censored.

The difference? Hicks challenged his audiences to examine their assumptions; Clay pandered, substituting the venting of his audience's petty frustrations for actual insight.

(You can guess the rest: Hicks was under-appreciated in his lifetime, although many comedians now consider him one of the greatest comics ever. Clay, meanwhile, wallowed in obvious generalizations and became an instant millionaire, although everyone felt dirty in the morning. The happy ending is that while Clay's career declines, Hicks' work is steadily gaining popularity. So even though he's dead, Hicks is still getting better gigs.)

So if *Dilbert* is our favorite comic strip, what does that say about us?

Evidently, the corporate domination of American life has a major downside, perhaps especially for the very employees whom one might presume would benefit the most.

Millions of people are frustrated on a daily basis. They'd do something about it if they knew how. That's a big deal. It's precisely that sort of widespread discontent that drives social changes.

To its credit, *Dilbert* does an outstanding job of making its audience laugh at their troubles. Too bad its talented creator never addresses the larger causes of their frustration.

"The real story of Dilbert is the basic disregard for his dignity as a human being, which is the biggest problem in workplaces generally," Scott Adams said in a 1996 interview with *Inc.* magazine.

The key to almost every *Dilbert* character is simple: a futile desire for esteem.

Beyond Dilbert, co-workers Alice and Wally are even worse off: overworked, quick-tempered, lonely, and bitter. The nameless Boss is both incompetent and power-hungry. Ratbert will never be loved because he's just a rat. Tina the tech writer is utterly unable to gain respect. And so on.

If this is what we're laughing at, that means a lot of us feel isolated and unable to improve our situation.

Adams clearly knows he's massaging the powerless. In the *Dilbert* newsletter, where Adams addresses his readers directly, he dubs them "Dogbert's New Ruling Class." That's funny, but only as a sardonic play on the obvious impotence of his readers.

The same joke is repeated often, as Adams ironically refers to his fans as "inexplicably attractive," "frighteningly intelligent," etc.

It's a lot like the shtick Rush Limbaugh uses to jack his audience's collective ego, and it works. There's even a secret hand signal that *Dilbert* buffs can use to mock non-initiates in their presence. (Make a fist and wag your little finger. Long story. Not important.)

Dilbert readers apparently do a lot of fist-making. Adams once asked his fans to select their top three annoying business practices. Almost 4,200 votes were cast, so roughly 1,400 people apparently voted. The top two vote-getters? "Idiots promoted to management" and "Being forced to work with idiots." Those two responses alone received over 1,560 votes, meaning that virtually every single respondent expressed contempt for co-workers, and more than 160 *Dilbert* fans—over 10 percent—considered it worth two votes out of three.

That's funny. It's also sad.

But it's predictable, because nowhere in Dilbertland are deeper problems of corporate behavior ever addressed. Instead, Dilbert's difficulties are solely the result of personality conflicts and individual incompetence.

In short, Adams strongly implies that the real problem in the typical workplace is relatively simple: other people.

Surprisingly, Adams' newsletter is largely devoted to playfully but relentlessly encouraging animosity and loathing toward co-workers, management, and the population at large. A typical survey question for his readers was: "If you had a chance to hit your boss in the back of the head with one of the following objects, with no risk of getting caught, which would you choose?" Regular features include humorous stories of encounters with moronic "Induhviduals" (Adams' term for stupid people and/or non-*Dilbert* readers), an "Enemies List" of disliked pop-culture icons, and even snide answers to stupid e-mail questions from readers themselves.

Venting pent-up hostility is Adams' favorite note, and he plays it as hard as he can.

His newest book, *The Dilbert Future*, is subtitled "Thriving on Stupidity in the 21st Century." Previous titles include *Always Postpone Meetings with Time-Wasting Morons, Clues for the Clueless* and *It's Obvious You Won't Survive By Your Wits Alone.*

It's clever. It's funny. It's also the same joke repeated over and over.

"Humor-wise, the best types of thoughts and emotions are the ones that you wouldn't want to confess, such as greed, envy, pettiness, disdain, selfishness and the like."

—Scott Adams, *Dilbert* Newsletter #10, February 1996

This focus on the worst aspects of individual behavior allows a lot of damaging corporate assumptions and behaviors to pass unexamined.

Adams' approach to the issue of downsizing is a good example.

As regular *Dilbert* readers know, Catbert, the evil Human Resources director, often toys with helpless personnel before firing them capriciously.

Adams has written that like most felines, Catbert "looks harmless and cute and he doesn't care if you live or die." (*Dilbert* Newsletter #4, January 1995.) Placing such a character in Human Resources is genuinely funny.

But as a result, Catbert's actions are attributed not to position, but to personality.

Never mind that the entire point of Human Resources (a phrase worthy of much derision, reducing as it does all of humankind to mere mineral status) is to maximize worker output with a minimum of expense. When H.R. people push fellow employees out the door, they're not trying to be evil; they're just doing their job. Any H.R. director who doesn't will be pushed out the door as well.

As Adams should know, downsizing—which he has described supportively as companies simply "getting rid of jobs they don't need" (*Electronic Engineering Times*, June 17, 1996)—often occurs not because the workers aren't doing their jobs or the work isn't necessary, but to replace full-timers with temps to minimize benefit payouts, to reduce payroll prior to a potential takeover, or numerous other reasons that have nothing to do with improving efficiency or the lives of workers and customers.

Primary considerations here on Earth, these are side issues on planet *Dilbert*.

When downsizing is simply the result of Catbert's evil nature, the implied message is that the problem is personal, not structural, and that there's nothing really wrong with H.R. that another firing—of Catbert—wouldn't fix. Cruelty isn't viewed as the inevitable result of a system which discards people the moment they fail a cost-benefit analysis; cruelty is just caused by bad management technique.

Similarly, bad relations with co-workers are caused by bad co-workers, conflicts with management are caused by stupid managers, and so on.

To read *Dilbert* at length is to be told repeatedly that the entire world is filled with malicious idiots. Not only is that worldview misleading, it's also profoundly disabling. If the problems of corporate culture are structural, then there are millions of potential allies beyond the cubicle walls who might work together to solve those problems. If the problems are personal, then the difficulties of all the real Dilberts everywhere are just several million cases of isolated bad luck.

No wonder the people who read *Dilbert* feel powerless. The strip actually contributes directly and constantly to making them feel that way.

That's just tragic. The strip's enormous popularity is itself overwhelming proof of the structural nature of the need to change the way corporations conduct themselves.

Writers interviewing Adams often ask the same question that occurs to *Dilbert* fans when they realize their boss likes the strip too: If this strip is so radical, then why does management like it so much? Why do CEOs buy his business videos, praise his books, and pay him top dollar to visit their corporate meetings?

The answer: *Dilbert* is simply not a radical critique. But then, it was never intended to be.

Adams, who holds an economics degree and an M.B.A., shares Wall Street's worldview and strategies to an extent that would surprise many of his readers.

> "I knew I wanted to make as much money as I could, and I always figured I would make it by doing something entre-preneurial. I had several models in mind. The one I liked best involved making some kind of intellectual product and then selling it over and over.... I finally hit on *Dilbert*, which was very much in the make-one-sell-many mold."
>
> —Scott Adams, on his passion for cartooning (*Inc.* magazine, July 1996)

Notice that Dilbert's most common problems are dis-tractions—micromanagement, meetings, co-workers, assignment changes, etc.—that prevent him from get-ting work done. Dilbert would be so much happier if only he could focus completely on the task at hand.

This assumption—Productivity equals Bliss—doesn't threaten corporate goals, but reinforces them. How much would major corporations pay to have their employees subtly indoctrinated with this ethic—by, say, a cartoon—on a daily basis?

Productivity equals Bliss is also the paradigm underlying the *Dilbert* management books, which fault corporate executives not for knowingly causing harm to customers, the environment, or even their own employees, but only for inadvertently lowering efficiency and harming the bottom line.

As mentioned, Adams is on record judging downsizing not by its impact on the workers' well-being, but on the company's. The profit motive is primary, superseding actual human needs. That's an odd belief system for an artist widely considered to be a leading critic of dehumanizing business practices.

That's why so many major newspapers are perfectly comfortable running *Dilbert* as the only comic in their daily business section.

As well they should be, as one of Adams' recent career moves reveals.

In 1995, Lockheed executives pleaded guilty to violating the Foreign Corrupt Practices Act after conspiring to bribe an Egyptian legislator with $1 million in order to get Egypt to buy almost $80 million worth of C-130 transport planes. Lockheed eventually paid a fine of almost $25 million and promised to create an internal ethics awareness training program.

As if. Lockheed still builds new planes that don't work—including the F-22, a $175 million long-range supersonic boondoggle whose current prototype will reportedly fly neither far nor fast—while selling old planes to dictatorships and laying off employees, including 1,600 in November 1996.

Meanwhile, guess who Lockheed hired to pitch in with their latest ethics program? Scott Adams.

For an undisclosed fee, Adams collaborated in creating Lockheed's "Ethics Challenge"—that name is not a joke—an interactive *Dilbert* board game which supposedly teaches everyone to play nice.

Since then, Lockheed has hired seven former Texas officials and contributed over $1 million to the campaigns of several others. Texas is privatizing the administration of services like food stamps and Medicaid to the poor. If Lockheed gets the contract, they'll pocket a cool $2 billion, although up to 5,000 current state employees will lose their jobs. Lockheed insists all the money they're tossing around Texas has nothing to do with trying to win the contract. And we all know how much Lockheed cares about the poor.

Adams hasn't said a public word about Lockheed that I can find. Either a) he doesn't know or care, which would be disheartening, seeing how he cashed their check in exchange for helping create an allegedly useful course in ethics; or b) he approves, which would be simply indefensible.

If he's not willing to blow that whistle, there's not much chance he'll throw his readers a lifeline by using his stage to examine and challenge the goals of the corporate world—especially not while he shares those ambitions so proudly.

> "If you can write on it, if it will hold a label, it's a prime target for licensing....You can't get to overexposure without getting to filthy rich first."
>
> —Scott Adams, on his goals for *Dilbert*
> (*Inc.* magazine, July 1996)

Until recently, almost half of the *Dilbert* newsletter (the part that wasn't expressing hostility) was just a long set of gratuitous plugs for *Dilbert* books, silk ties, suspenders, mugs, sweatshirts, caps, boxer shorts, yarmulkes, T-shirts, greeting cards, calendars, mouse pads, codpieces, plush toys, memo pads, and fetish gear. (OK, three of those don't belong. Just checking if you're paying attention.) Adams is making as much money as he possibly can.

This is not the voice of a white-collar revolution. By his own admission, Adams is making a buck while cleverly poking and teasing the cubicle prisoners and chortling over his own fortunate escape.

Of course *Dilbert* is popular. It vents anger while subtly sharing the operating assumptions of management. It's a safe way to thumb your nose at the boss without actually taking real action that might jeopardize, or improve, your own position.

Dilbert will make you laugh—a lot—at the weakness and stupidity of individual human beings. But that's all it will do.

Chapter 6

The Culture of Eye-Rolling Capitulation

The prolonged *Dilbert* craze makes anti-corporate impulses more visible and subdues them at the same time.

Some of *Dilbert*'s drumbeat assumptions get spelled out in the first chapter of *The Dilbert Future*. Under the heading of "Immutable Laws of Human Nature," Scott Adams lists three: "Stupidity." "Selfishness." "Horniness."

The third listing is just a dash of spice added to "Stupidity" and "Selfishness"—the key *Dilbert* themes. Once they're accepted as central and "immutable" human characteristics, then we're stuck. Only a naive fool would expect—or seek—anything much better.

To his dubious credit, Adams practices what *Dilbert* preaches.

In recent decades, a lot of contemporary art—from rock music to modern painting—has become fodder for the big guns of advertising. Scott Adams has led the way for a further innovation—the commercialization of "art" never intended as art. ("I think of myself as a businessman first and an artist second.") The meteoric use of *Dilbert* for commercial purposes is a new archetype—the loss of integrity that avowedly never existed.

Adams has gone out of his way to say that he isn't worried about compromising his principles. "I never had any integrity," Adams told the *Washington Post* (October 5, 1995). "This was always meant to be a business. My background is business school, so I can't imagine not commercializing something."

This is precisely where the much-vaunted imagination of Scott Adams hits its own cubicle wall. *I can't imagine not commercializing something.*

Dilbert is a powerful symbol in a way that none of its various hypesters acknowledge. *Dilbert* and Adams—sensational product and insatiable multimillionaire—symbolize inability to imagine resisting the priorities of a corporatized status quo. The line between artistic expression and commercial promotion, neo-art and hyper-advertising, is not just thin and broken. The disappearance of that line is a fading memory.

"In short," writes *Village Voice* columnist Leslie Savan, "we're living the sponsored life." She points out: "The sponsored life is born when commercial culture sells our own experiences back to us. It grows as those experiences are then reconstituted inside us, mixing the most intimate processes of individual thought with commercial values, rhythms, and expectation." And, she could have added, *lack* of expectation.

The degrading of standards—of what we expect and are willing to accept—commonly leaves us with flimsy dissent. If our actions seem faithful enough, it's not necessary that we become true believers in the corporate gods. It is sufficient to genuflect and keep silent at the appropriate times; semiprivate eye-rolling is generally permissible. The workplace and the ad place almost demand ineffectual snippets of cynical mutterings from all but the most credulous of us. "The ironic reflex," Savan calls it—"the most popular postmodern response to advertising's dominant role in our culture."

In her book *The Sponsored Life*, Savan presents a description of TV watchers that is quite relevant to *Dilbert* readers:

> Irony has become a hallmark of the sponsored life because it provides a certain distance from the frustration inherent in commercial correctness. For some time now the people raised on television, the baby boomers and the "Generation Xers" that followed, have mentally adjusted the set, as it were, in order to convince themselves that watching is cool. They may be doing exactly what their parents do—but they do it *differently*. They take in TV with a Lettermanesque wink, and they like it when it winks back....The winkers believe that by rolling their collective eyes when they watch TV they can control *it*, rather than letting it control them. But unfortunately, as a defense against the power of advertising, irony is a leaky condom—in fact, it's the same old condom that advertising brings over every night. A lot of ads have learned that to break through to the all-important boomer and Xer markets they have to be as cool, hip, and ironic as the target audience likes to think of itself as being. That requires at least the pose of opposition to commercial values. The cool commercials...flatter us by saying we're too cool to fall for commercial values, and therefore cool enough to want their product.

Dilbert—particularly in book form—deftly threads this tried-and-lucrative '90s needle. Adams pursues a mass audience while repeatedly striving to flatter it as distinct from the mass audience of "Induhviduals." He lampoons commercial charlatanism while implementing his own brand for maximum return. And he winks often enough to risk eye-strain.

Savan's delineation of present-day ad "winkers" is a snug fit for Scott Adams and the appreciative audience he has been able to cultivate: They "have enthusiastically embraced the artifice, even the manipulativeness, of advertising as an essential paradox of modern life, a paradox that is at the crux of their own identity."

<hr />

In the late 1990s, the frenzied *Dilbert* marketing ventures may seem like logical business transactions. But that's because more impressive talents have so often undergone prostitution in recent decades.

When the Rolling Stones went on tour in 1981 under the logo of Jovan perfumes, and later for Budweiser beer, the willingness of a superstar rock band to emblazon itself with a product far afield from music helped normalize the process across the mass-cultural board. Back then, there was a potentially glaring contrast to be perceived between some earlier content ("Street Fighting Man") and new commercial affect ("King of Beers").

But we got used to contradictions that came to seem complementary. And more and more, the door swung both ways. If famously rebellious rock artists could promote brands of perfume and beer, then big-time

© Clay Butler

environmental despoilers could present themselves as humanitarian.*

By the time *Dilbert* became a big media success, many companies were accustomed to paying for symbols that—one way or another—prettied up their images. To the point of absurdity.

DuPont, a leading chemical contaminator, produced TV ads featuring merrily clapping seals. The same timber companies involved in rapacious clear-cutting put out "plant a tree" ads. Chevron spent several hundred thousand dollars on an ad campaign hyping its butterfly preservation efforts, which cost the company $5,000 per year. Such "greenwashing" became routine on so-called

---

*"The more hawkish a company's record, the more mawkish its self-portrait," Leslie Savan wrote in 1985. She continued: "In its first national TV ads, Dow Chemical is 'repositioning.' Like napalm and Agent Orange victims, Dow says it got burned during Vietnam and claims to have hightailed it away from the weapons business (though Greenpeace, for one, calls Dow among the country's worst polluters). Meanwhile, Dow has acquired companies that make cleansers and lozenges, and so wants to get closer to the customer. To introduce born-again Dow, one ad has a mop-o'-curls college kid writing: 'Just got back from my Dow interview. Sounds like my kind of research. Finding new ways to grow more food, ways to help sick people. I'm going to go for it, Dad.' (Cut to Dad reading the letter, gulping hard.) 'I'm going to try to make you proud.' In another spot, graduating 'Cindy' confides: 'I never understood when Mom made me clean my plate because there were places where kids were starving. Now I'm about to walk into a Dow laboratory to work on new ways to grow more and better grain... I can't wait!' Who better to absolve Dow than its old nemesis, college students? How better to tell students it's okay to go for the bread than by insisting they're going for the grain? Kids forgive Dow, Dow forgives kids, Mom and Dad trust Dow. And we're all sanctioned not to worry."

public TV by the early 1990s. More than a dozen corporate polluters—including BASF, Goodyear and
Mobil—polished their images by underwriting nature
shows.

On the mass-culture front, *Rolling Stone* epitomized the
trends. In the summer of 1987, *Rolling Stone* became the
"official magazine" of the nationally televised Coors
International Bicycle Classic. The Coors beer company—
notorious for its owners' anti-union policies, racial bias
and massive funding of right-wing outfits like the
Heritage Foundation—found in *Rolling Stone* a willing
partner in a mutual makeover.

While the magazine could be made to seem more
respectable for advertisers, Savan explained, Coors could
buy a new likeness too: "Adolph Coors Co.'s reputation
as racist, antigay, and in general the enemy of the good
fight everywhere, scares off concerned guzzlers. But by
spending $12 per barrel of beer on marketing, more than
any other brewery, Coors is putting on the centrist
lifestyle."

A decade later, *Dilbert* was a handy new tool for huge
firms in the computer industry to shatter the perception
that they might be corporate giants of the cubicle sort.
Companies such as Intel and Computer Associates
International, eager to lease the *Dilbert* logo, found a
bargain—a winking kind of Good Dilberting Seal of
Approval—much cheaper than actually doing something
to improve conditions for employees. And for marketing
purposes, what could be better than using a quintessential
anti-corporate symbol to boost a corporate image?

Corporate *Dilbert* is as welcoming as corporate rock.
Leslie Savan described the attraction: "It's easy to accept

corprock, because it seems knee-jerk idealistic and unhip not to.... But the belief that corprock is harmless is soggy. It gives some susceptible fans permission to think it's cool

---

"But if you can't be rich, the next best thing is to be smug and cynical."
—Scott Adams, *The Dilbert Principle*, p. 125

---

to work for a corp, and question it less. Mostly, it confirms what young careerists want to hear anyway—that they can be hip and gimme-gimme at the same time."

Wired magazine devoted a dozen pages of its May 1997 issue to a "Special Report" titled "CORPORATE REBELS." It began with a pair of pages mocked up as a revolutionary poster, with proletarians waving picket signs. "Think For Yourself," one said. "No Business As Usual," another demanded.

While the everyman Dilbert is daily trapped in cubicles and condemned to failure, the "corporate rebels" celebrated by *Wired* have been able to transcend the cubicles. *Wired's* heroes are exceptions proving that the rule of corporations need not be inept or oppressive.

If you're one of the world's Dilberts, then *Wired's* favorite rebels can serve as idols who have stormed the corporate gates and triumphed. Although you probably aren't okay, they are—impressively so.

"Inflexible bureaucracy, top-down management, tight-ly regulated industries, monopoly—these are the tired remnants of the old corporate world order," *Wired* pro-claimed in big type. "The new economy demands new thinking, yet the why-fix-it-if-it-ain't-broken attitude often prevails among CEOs who are too myopic to notice that the market has evolved, let alone to envision how it will look in five years. So change often comes from within, from independent thinkers who see old problems with new eyes."

With the focus on how technology and smarts can gain market share, other matters are peripheral or invisi-ble. *Wired* cheers for profitable innovation; Scott Adams disdains the lack of it. The only specter of righteous rebellion involves a passion for bumping up the bottom line.

"Those who break the shackles of business as usual—corporate rebels—set the pace for the next millennium," *Wired* declared. "They are iconoclasts who question the status quo, cut through red tape, and challenge their bosses to greatness.... The smarter companies tap the uprising within, creating ways to turn the steam of the rebel into the fuel that drives the business."

Permanently nonplussed, Dilbert can hardly catch a glimpse of a scenario in which his "steam" could turn the firm's mighty turbines. Dilbert would like to picture himself among those who "challenge their bosses to greatness." But what would the "greatness" be?

To *Wired*, and to Scott Adams, the great rebels over-come barriers that prevent them from better serving owners and investors. Dilbert, the cartoon man, is light years from such an achievement. But, like someone watching *Lifestyles of the Rich and Famous* for the price of the TV and electricity, Dilbert might very well thumb through *Wired* and dream of being one of its heroes. Like, for instance, Ted Selker—*Wired*'s lead "Corporate Rebel" in 1997—the research fellow at IBM who earned the headline "Rebel Without a Pause."

The wonderful fact was that Selker had a cause, as the *Wired* caption explained. "CAUSE: Battled engineering and manufacturing skeptics to create the trackpoint, the knobby red pointing device that helped boost sales of IBM's ThinkPad portable PC."

Wow! That's a rebel for you.

Right behind him came other *Wired* heroes: The wealthy founder of International Discount Telecommunications Corp.; the vice president of the Satellite Communications Group at Motorola; the designer of "a radical companywide internal network" for the U S West conglomerate; an innovator of on-line stock brokerage...

By now, we've run across similar stories many times in news media: A scrappy inventor took on the business establishment and made a fortune. An engineer battled myopic bosses to develop a great new product. A brilliant computer nerd overcame entrenched foes and now heads the firm.

Nowhere is this media tone more fervent than at *Wired*, which went over the 300,000 circulation mark in early 1996, barely three years after its launch. The ornate magazine is quite influential with an affluent readership—including many journalists—eager to keep tabs on cutting-edge computer trends. Its editors provide a hospitable environment for big sleek ads from outfits like

© Tom Tomorrow

Intel, Sony, Lucent Technologies, Microsoft, Smith Barney, Panasonic and U.S. Robotics.

Wired mingles technical updates and human-interest features with ardor for companies now gaining unprecedented control over systems of mass communication. Why worry about such matters when the ad revenue is pouring in?

With grimly laughable pretenses, *Wired* glorifies a procession of "rebels" for struggling to persuade a corporate hierarchy to let them generate profits. In a vague echo of New Age platitudes, these crusades are likened to the sacred quest for human freedom.

The limits aren't hard to discern. When the magazine's corporate parent, Wired Ventures, tried to attract investment capital in 1996, it boasted that "none of the company's employees is represented by a labor union."

Of course, according to some mainstream news outlets, *Wired* itself qualifies as a corporate rebel. The *New York Times* has dubbed *Wired* "the icon of the Internet generation." The newspaper declared: "The genius of *Wired* is that it makes the Digital Revolution a self-fulfilling prophesy, both illuminating this new sub-culture and promoting it."

The corporate kings are dead. Long live the corporate kings. The new ideology of business-as-upheaval is "a way of justifying and exercising power that has absolutely nothing to do with the 'conformity' and the 'establishment' so vilified by the countercultural idea," writes Thomas Frank. "The management theorists and 'leadership' charlatans of the Information Age don't waste their time prattling about hierarchy and regulation, but about disorder, chaos, and the meaninglessness of inherited rules."

Just about anything goes if higher profits seem a plausible result. Managers who insist they want to be challenged don't mean they want to encourage union organizing and worker solidarity—but they do mean that fluidity can be more productive than rigidity.

The marketplace wars cannot be fought effectively with corporate soldiers lined up like redcoats. Better strategies could require leaving tradition behind. In many office settings, a new informality may now be the formal necessity. And if free-flowing workplace styles can be rhetorically likened to freedom and self-actualization, then so much the better.

The mass market of the 1990s has woven a curtain that divides the present from passé idealism. Vibrant creativity is worth getting excited about only if a sales path can be cleared for it. In 1997, when a carefully selected portion of Elton John's song "Rocket Man" made it onto an AT&T commercial, or when Kurt Vonnegut did a TV spot for Discover Card, few people raised their eyebrows. By now, just about everything or everyone is assumed to have a price.*

For every synthetic rebel, hailed as heroic in the service of the corporation, there must be many thousands of

---

*The dead, of course, are the least likely to complain. On April 30, 1997, the first page of the New York Times section about "The Arts" revealed that "Thirty Years After His Death, Che Guevara Has New Charisma." That small headline ran under a bigger one: "FROM REBEL TO POP ICON." We should all be so lucky. Typically,

Dilberts. High achievers are laudable and all that, but the multitudes are requisite corporate materiel. The entrepreneur hero is a god who remains distinct from the vast numbers of somewhat faithful schlumps, the Dilberts, the bored and stressed Joes and Joans—the workers and buyers who make the glorious profits possible.

And our best consuming days, presumably, lie ahead of us—bleak matchups of what Thomas Frank calls "human gullibility and iron corporate will."

➤•◄

It was appropriate that the Fox TV network poured development money into a *Dilbert* sitcom in 1997. The comic strip resembles many situation comedies on television—quirky irreverence on a very short leash, never getting out of hand.

In the standard sitcom and other TV programing, as Mark Crispin Miller has commented, "contemptuous passivity reflects directly on the viewer who watches it with precisely the same attitude. TV seems to flatter the inert skepticism of its own audience, assuring them they can do no better than to stay right where they are, rolling

---

Guevara's face is on a limited-edition Swatch with a watchband that says "REVOLUCION" in big letters. "The Communist rebel chief's characteristic beard, beret and fatigues have inspired a Che look-alike contest designed to sell skis," the *Times* reported. The assistant product manager for the New York distributor of Fischer's Revolution skis provided a suitable quote: "We felt that the Che image—just the icon and not the man's doings—represented what we wanted: revolution, extreme change." The *Times*, for good measure, added that in the three decades since Guevara's death, "his image has become more vivid, complex and commercial."

their eyes in feeble disbelief. And yet such apparent flattery of our viewpoint is in fact a recurrent warning not to rise above this slack, derisive gaping."

At first, "it seems that it is only those eccentric others whom TV belittles," Miller wrote in his 1988 book *Boxed In.* "Each time some deadpan tot on a sitcom responds to his frantic mom with a disgusted sigh, or whenever the polished anchorman punctuates his footage of 'extremists' with a look that speaks his well-groomed disapproval, or each time Johnny Carson comments on some 'unusual' behavior with a wry sidelong glance into our living rooms, we are being flattered with a gesture of inclusion, the wink that tells us, 'We are in the know.'" But the put-down routines discourage straying from the herd.

Major TV networks are good at marketing mild audacity, subservient to those who wield the big checks. Even on the rare occasions when a program starts out by pushing hard on some boundaries, it's likely to grow tame if it remains on the air.

In autumn 1996, humorist Bob Harris wrote about what became of *Saturday Night Live:*

Perhaps the most amusing thing about *Saturday Night Live* is that the stuff they did twenty years ago is still funnier than the crap they're churning out today....

Why is the show so unfunny? One word: class.

Genuine laughter is an involuntary neural response, requiring at least minimal comfort and empathy between the performer and audience.

For most folks here in the real world, it's a struggle to get by. That's more true now than in the '70s.

And notice that *all* of the popular old *SNL* characters—the Coneheads, the cheeseburger cooks, the Killer Bees, Emily Litella, Todd and Lisa, the "wild and crazy guys," etc.—were outsiders, vulnerable and struggling. Even the Land Shark had to plead with his victims before attacking.

Not surprisingly, most of the writing staff was working class. Their world and ours connected. Even the hosts— Ralph Nader, Julian Bond, Jimmy Breslin, etc.—were often champions of the little guy, as were musical guests like Patti Smith, Gil Scott-Heron, and Frank Zappa.

Times change.

Today's 25-year-old comedy writers were 9 when Reagan was elected. Many are Harvard grads who chose TV writing instead of getting an M.B.A. NBC is now owned by GE, one of the biggest, nastiest defense contractors on the planet.

Predictably, *SNL*'s most notable recent hosts have been Lamar Alexander and Steve Forbes—raw meat to the old writers; royalty in the new order.

Disdain for women, minorities, and the poor fairly oozed from a recent show:

Impersonations of Johnny Carson and Phil Donahue were performed with unironic, admiring reverence. However, an ad parody for "Russell & Tate: Attorneys" featured stereotyped jive-talking blacks working as lawyers. Get it? Apparently the very idea of lower-class blacks pursuing a white-collar career is itself a source of humor. Can racism be more blunt?

Meanwhile, the only working-class white character was a boorish housewife with freakishly distended breasts, who shouted at neighbors and insulted innocent trick-or-treaters. In most TV comedy, poor Caucasians are portrayed and referred to as "white trash"—intellectually, physically, or emotionally inferior to richer white people.

Of course, there's no such phrase as "black trash" or "red trash." People with those colorations are presumed to be poor. "White trash" connotes economic failure only notable for the color of skin. It's an explicitly racist term, although few people seem to care.

Female sexuality is a real problem on *SNL*. In this episode, gratuitous mentions of female circumcision—which the writers must not know is forced genital mutilation akin to perpetual rape—appeared in several sketches as a running gag.

Yipes.

Rapper Dr. Dre was the musical guest. He fit right in, rationalizing his multimillionaire status with a chorus of gotta get that money baby, gotta get that cash. Megadittos.

So much for empathy with the audience.

I also recently attended a taping of *SNL*'s rival, *MAD TV*, owned by Rupert Murdoch, the richest man in Southern California.

It was even worse. Laugh at this:

Elderly people kept in cages like animals. A white couple patiently waiting as a stupid black Southerner gives directions. A big guy shoving a midget. Partygoers openly mocking a grieving man whose wife has just died.

The working class—the audience at home, remember —was represented by a poor uneducated couple (Southerners again, of course) so addicted to pornography that the husband works literally sucking excrement. An inspired metaphor for the abuse of unskilled labor, perhaps? Nah, just a chance to be gross.

At its best, *Saturday Night Live* wasn't too subversive. But it had some joie de vivre, punch, and humor that embraced humanity instead of ridiculing it. All of which faded away long ago. What remained was another triumph for corporate culture.

CHAPTER 7

REDUCING STRESS AND BOOSTING PROFITS

Early on, this book quotes a flip comment by *Newsweek*—circa 1996—about the grim pressures of the workplace: "At least we'll have *Dilbert* around for counsel and comfort. If your HMO limits you to one mental-health session per annum, your vacation is downsized and your coffee break is eliminated, *Dilbert* will be one tonic you can always afford."

And we thought that was a joke.

In mid-1997, readers of the Sunday paper in San Francisco found an announcement in big letters on the front of the color comics: "DILBERT HAS MOVED. Please visit him in our Career Search Section." The editors of the *Examiner* had decided to put *Dilbert*, in its full color format, on the first page of Career Search news. So, on June 8, *Dilbert* appeared just under the section's lead story—about on-the-job burnout—with a headline promising an explanation of "Ways to vaccinate yourself against the job stress 'epidemic.'"

The article provided ideas for how to cope with nearly unbearable working conditions. Among the article's suggestions: "Get the stress out of your system through exercise, yoga or massage... Find ways to 'switch gears' after work... Take mini-breaks at work... Find ways to integrate a sense of play throughout your work day, such as through *Dilbert* cartoons, funny pens or desk toys. Personalize your work space with photos, flowers and other items that have a relaxing influence..."

To a large extent, the newspaper article was based on a press release from Kaiser Permanente, the largest HMO in California. That release, dated May 1997 and titled "Taking the Stress Out of Being Stressed Out," began:

> Walk into any workplace, and you'll find a dog-eared *Dilbert* cartoon taped to a wall somewhere.
>
> No matter how offbeat Scott Adams makes the comic strip, his readers continue to say, "That's just like my company."
>
> In real life, many of us are Dilbert. And statistics about on-the-job stress prove it. According to the U.S. Department of Labor, the workplace is the greatest single source of stress, no matter what you do or how much you earn. The New York-based American Institute of Stress reports that as many as 75 to 90 percent of visits to physicians are related to stress—at a price tag to American businesses of $200 to $300 billion a year.

The spin was fairly overt, with Kaiser pitching its stress-reduction program to appeal to corporate heavies in a position to buy group health plans. It wasn't enough to cite the "price tag to American businesses." The news release put a fine point on the matter: "Kaiser Permanente is taking bold steps to hold down these costs and help employees handle their on-the-job stress at the same time."

A clinical psychologist, Kris Ludwigsen, Ph.D., was credited with "setting up group sessions for Kaiser Permanente members who need help handling stress. Part of the members' treatment consists of talking with co-workers or supervisors to help identify the causes of stress. These actions enable members to learn how to handle their stress while they're in the thick of it—on the job."

Notice the emphasis: The "group sessions" (a frugal contrast to individual ones) are for workers who "need help handling stress" and can benefit from "treatment"— part of which involves talking with "co-workers or supervisors" to get help in identifying "the causes of stress." But there's no mention of then trying to alter those "causes of stress." Instead, the process will "enable members to learn how to handle their stress." Got oppressive working conditions? *Get used to it.*

To underscore that its "bold steps" could mean big savings for companies, Kaiser quoted Ludwigsen, the clinical psychologist who has learned how to talk the talk that can be music to management ears: "We're trying to help people identify self-empowering strategies that they can use to deal with their stress, rather than file for disability or workmen's compensation."

Now that's a "self-empowering strategy."

———※◆※———

Much that gets said openly these days—without a trace of embarrassment—testifies to just how degraded public sensibilities have become. It's revealing that Scott Adams, in a spring 1997 interview with *Editor & Pub-*

lisher, felt free to say on the record: "Actually, my only intention is for people to transfer their money to me." His willingness to volunteer such a comment says much more about the society we now live in than it does about one individual.

Obviously, Adams has gauged that such a statement risks no backlash that he cares about. He's been making those kind of comments for years—as in his 1995 declaration to the *Washington Post*, "I never had any integrity. This was always meant to be a business." The newspaper was hardly inclined to make a big deal out of the remark.

In her 1997 autobiography *Personal History*, the longtime owner of the Washington Post Company makes clear how admirable she finds the obsession to pile up as much personal wealth as possible. One of Katharine Graham's most effusive and affectionate portrayals is her paean to Warren Buffett, corporate raider par excellence. In a book that renders many business titans as near-saints, Buffett—who's ranked as the country's second-richest man—is served up as a cross between Mister Greenjeans and Albert Einstein, with puckish zest for acquiring billions. Buffett's interests are singular, Graham explains with adoration: "What he loves is business—thinking and reading and talking about business."

Four decades after C. Wright Mills wrote *The Power Elite*, some changes are unmistakable. Silicon Valley startups and Microsoft, along with thousands of leveraged buyouts and initial public offerings, symbolize how new big money can crowd out the old. But Mills attacked a powerful core of corporate idolatry that remains: *Dilbert* may spoof it and *Wired* may tweak it, but both are adherents to what Mills called "the true higher immorality of our time...the organized irresponsibility that is today the most important characteristic of the American system of corporate power."

—*The Dilbert Principle*, p. 59

In this court of "higher immorality," Dilbert is a jester who elicits some chuckles while kissing the sovereigns and nodding to the corporate throne. The respect is mutual. (*Business Week*: "CEOs hang him on the wall.") Spoofing the foibles of the corporate monarchy with a manner of impish ingratiation, Scott Adams and his cartoonish alter egos set examples for those who "are Dilbert."

While capturing some absurd aspects of the '90s office, *Dilbert* and Adams also provide us with refracted role models for how to respond to that absurdity. They—and we—adapt to the hard-wired economy. Intel inside. Our assent gives more permanence to what's increasingly cited as unchangeable.

Nihilism easily welcomes corporate rule, and vice versa. The cycle is powerful. "The higher immorality can neither be narrowed to the political sphere nor understood as primarily a matter of corrupt men in fundamentally sound institutions," Mills wrote. "Political corruption is one aspect of a more general immorality; the level of moral sensibility that now prevails is not merely a matter of corrupt men. The higher immorality is a systematic feature of the American elite; its general acceptance is an essential feature of the mass society."

People shape themselves to fit the criteria of corporate America—"and are thus made by the criteria, the social premiums that prevail." Most of us can find no viable option other than fitting in the grooves made available by the reigning political economy.

"In the corporate era," C. Wright Mills wrote, "economic relations become impersonal—and the executive feels less personal responsibility. Within the corporate worlds of business, war-making and politics, the private conscience is attenuated—and the higher immorality is institutionalized. It is not merely a question of a corrupt administration in corporation, army, or state; it is a feature of the corporate rich, as a capitalist stratum, deeply intertwined with the politics of the military state."

For all we know, the projects that Dilbert and Wally and Alice work on—grinding their teeth at the office's stupid inefficiencies—involve operating systems for guided missiles. Actually, in a Sunday comic that appeared in December 1994, the Boss asked Dilbert: "Has your team finished engineering the new missile guidance chip?"

Or maybe Dilbert and his colleagues are working on management software for a global web of apparel factories in places like Honduras and Vietnam and Indonesia, where sweatshops provide optimum profit margins. Or perhaps they're getting the bugs out of nuclear-reactor software. Or complex public-relations algorithms for a firm that dumps toxic chemicals in areas where poor people live.

Since the end-use of products and the ultimate results of labor are not on the table or in the air for discussion, we're left with the matter of efficiency. That's supposed to be a vital goal. But in many cases, given the destruction and pain caused by what's being produced, we'd be better off with more inept bureaucracy, not less.

What's always around is the alluring notion of rearranging the corporate furniture—sometimes literally—to set things right. Such scenarios bring no deep changes.

"In economic and political institutions the corporate rich now wield enormous power," Mills wrote, "but they have never had to win the moral consent of those over whom they hold this power." Rather than causing a sense of public crisis, key aspects of the dominant immorality "have been matters of a creeping indifference and a silent hollowing out." Corporate standards ooze into much personal space: "Money is the one unambiguous criterion of success, and such success is still the sovereign American value.... It is not only that men want money; it is that their very standards are pecuniary."

So Scott Adams is in step because his "very standards are pecuniary." He believes in profit as "the one unambiguous criterion of success." The odious values he satirizes in *Dilbert* are the same ones he embraces in marketing the *Dilbert* product.

Workers are consumers, and (usually) vice versa. But lowered expectations exclude us from having a say about *how* we produce as well as *what* we produce—and what kind of priorities should guide each step of economic activity.

—»•«—

To imagine is the first step toward other possibilities. But *Dilbert* is about contracted options, not expansive ones.

Yet *Dilbert* has convinced many that it occupies ground at the far end of opposition to what corporate America is about. In this hoodwinking process—a furthering of what Mills referred to as "a silent hollowing out"—the destruction of imagination involves funneling creativity toward the corporately useful. This is just one more way that corporate culture gets the last laugh.

Dilbert has come to play a classic celebrity role, with both its main character and its creator appearing on a spectrum of glossy magazine covers. The distracting functions are especially poignant. Dilbert has become far better known than many of the most powerful magnates who harm thousands of lives with the stroke of a pen, whether the top AT&T executive ordering massive layoffs or the CEO of Shell signing off on the oil company's collusion with the murderous military regime in Nigeria.

"The power elite is not so noticeable as the celebrities, and often does not want to be; the 'power' of the professional celebrity is the power of distraction." Those words, written by Mills in the late '50s, ring true today—and perhaps never more so than in the context of *Dilbert*.

The power of distraction is evident with Hollywood stars. But at least they're understood to be entertainers without direct relevance to the stresses and strains of the workplace. They generally don't claim to be addressing the conditions under which most of us spend forty or so hours a week.

Dilbert is different—a celebrity now grouped among the nation's most fascinating and influential "people" by magazines like *Time* and *Newsweek*. As a cartoon figure, Dilbert has gained enormous stature by dint of the claim that he is a trenchant symbol of our everyday work lives. For news media, *Dilbert* has become a marvelously narrow question that answers itself profoundly.

Entertainment Weekly, January 31, 1997: "Is this nebbishy comic-strip hero worth all the adulation? Frankly, yes. In nailing the Kafkaesque world of office existence, with its petty humiliations, meaningless jargon, and spirit-shriveling tedium, Adams captures the lunacy of our little lives just as surely as *Pogo* or *Peanuts* or *Doonesbury* did in their primes." Dilbert is a celebrity whose power to distract is greatly heightened by the widely propagated belief that he is both fiction and reality, both satirical emblem and literal statement about how working people perceive their daily lives.

As a celebrated rebel, Dilbert has galvanized notions of what rebellion might entail. Like a hyper-charged magnet, he has drawn to him the anger and resentment, the petty and profound, the frustrations and the rage that permeate so much that's involved with making a living these days. And *Dilbert* has channeled many of those ongoing emotions into a cul-de-sac.

On Dilbert Lane, to rebel is to find new ways to pioneer conformity and win accolades for doing so. Going around in circles, there is everything to gain in the monetary sense—trumpeted as the only sense that makes much.

⮞◦⮜

The big-selling *Dogbert's Top Secret Management Handbook*, published in 1996, was a smooth vehicle for Scott Adams to cruise along—with uninterrupted contempt for ethical concerns—under the vicarious guise of putting out a sardonic Machiavellian manual for hardhearted managers.

One way or another, Adams routinely skirts along this campy edge, inviting projections and raking in megabucks from each side of the management-worker divide. He's merrily cashing in on both ends of the ethical/anti-ethical dichotomy.

Dogbert's Top Secret Management Handbook can be read cover-to-cover in this context. It's replete with statements like: "Leadership isn't only about selfish actions. It's also about empty, meaningless expressions." At one level, Scott Adams is getting richer by deploring such attitudes; simultaneously he's getting richer by implementing them.

CHAPTER 8

"MAYBE YOUR ODDS
ARE A MATTER
OF YOUR CONTROL"

"Industrially produced fiction has become one of the primary shapers of our emotions and our intellect in the twentieth century," Ariel Dorfman observed in the early 1980s, a decade after co-authoring *How to Read Donald Duck*. He described an escalating dynamic in a multimedia world: "Although these [fictional] stories are supposed merely to entertain us, they constantly give us a secret education. We are not only taught certain styles of violence, the latest fashions, and sex roles by TV, movies, magazines, and comic strips; we are also taught how to succeed, how to love, how to buy, how to conquer, how to forget the past and suppress the future. We are taught, more than anything else, how not to rebel."

Denying that this situation exists is central to perpetuating it.

"We are taught, more than anything else, how not to rebel."

One of the best ways of teaching people how not to rebel is to offer plenty of ruts for fake rebellion. These slit trenches contain the runoff of frustration, ire and anguish that's part of daily life. We remain unduly impressed with the narrow media conduits.

"The overriding influence of this kind of fiction has been increasingly recognized," Dorfman notes, "and yet there has also been a tendency to avoid scrutinizing these mass media products too closely, to avoid asking the sort of hard questions that can yield disquieting answers. It is not strange that this should be so. The industry itself has declared time and again with great forcefulness that it is innocent, that no hidden motives or implications are lurking behind the cheerful faces it generates."

On the surface, the faces in *Dilbert* may be far from cheerful. "Dour-full" would seem to be more like it. And yet, downbeat and claustrophobic as the *Dilbert* world-view is, it dodges grimmer truths by identifying the key problems as either too humanly intrinsic to change ("we're all idiots") or so mechanical that someday things could get straightened out to the mutual benefit of owners and workers.

In any event, no need to disrupt the existing division of power and resources: The problems we face are either unalterably human or simply an absence of more efficient management techniques. In short, no need to question the essence of corporate power. On the big stuff—if only by omission—*Dilbert* is immersed in blithe optimism.

—————⟫•◦•⟪—————

A reality more somber than the glummest *Dilbert* episode comes into focus in Ariel Dorfman's book *The Empire's Old Clothes*:

Perhaps it is inevitable that the consumer should be treated as an infant, helpless and demanding, in societies such as ours. As a member of a democratic system, he has the right to vote and the even more important right and obligation to consume; but at the same time he is not really participating in the determination of his future or that of the world. People can be treated as children because they do not, in effect, control their own destiny. Even if they feel themselves to be utterly free, they are objectively vulnerable and dependent, passive in a world commandeered by others, a world where the messages they swallow have originated in other people's minds.

Faux rebellion and its cultural products tend to be depleting. At the end of the day there's not much left but exhaustion and the unpleasant prospect of going through it all again tomorrow. Nothing of genuine substance is supposed to change. That lets us off the hook: a hollow kind of cheeriness.

Edward S. Herman has criticized recent trends along this line, when people "take the status quo as given, fail to examine forms and structures of domination that underpin it, and provide no basis for analyzing or organizing to change the status quo." Writing in the January 1996 issue of Z Magazine, he added:

> The postmodernist celebration of the power of the individual and rejection of global models (and inferentially, global solutions to problems) has an even deeper perversity, in that it reinforces individualism at a time when collective resistance to corporate domination is the central imperative. The market consists of numerous corporations that organize and plan to achieve their narrow goals, and which have been steadily growing in size, glob-

al reach, and power.... Stemming the current market tide, and any future turnabout, is going to require organization, programs and strategies from below. In this context, could anything be more perverse politically and intellectually than a retreat to micro-analysis, the celebration of minor individual triumphs, and reliance on solutions based on individual actions alone?

....Pessimism and disillusionment have also led some to a further retreat, with an abandonment of the desire as well as hope for progressive change, and to a celebration of the status quo and the options it affords the individual. The postmodern celebration of popular culture as the locus of subversion and resistance ignores its increasing integration into the life-style and shopping mall world and takes the domination of consumer capitalism as a given.

A third of a century ago, scholar Herbert Marcuse saw *Dilbert* coming. "In this society," he wrote, "the productive apparatus tends to become totalitarian to the extent to which it determines not only the socially needed occupations, skills, and attitudes, but also individual needs and aspirations."

For the system, the individual Dilbert is not even a cog. The wavy-headed guy with the flippy tie is merely a tiny bolt on humongous corporate machinery—which severely circumscribes Dilbert's private world. What matters about the private Dilbert is what matters to the corporate system.

Like his colleagues, he's reduced to feeble wisecracks and asides, the gallows humor of a man sentenced to live the corporate life. For Dilbert, a sparse and antiseptic cubicle is minimum security.

The cyber-jargon and cyber-technology now pushing each other forward are symbols of how sour the dream of progress has turned; today's computerized office is a curdled replication of yesterday. Dilbert—and millions of men and women who identify with his workaday plight—are moving from disappointment toward fatalism.

> "The beauty of our current system of capitalism is that it legally discriminates against the two groups who are least likely to complain: stupid people, AKA Induhviduals, because they don't realize they're getting screwed; and lazy people, because protesting is like work. Unlike other forms of discrimination that are rightly outlawed, almost everyone agrees it's fair to discriminate against lazy and stupid people. It's a very stable system."
>
> —Scott Adams, *The Dilbert Future*, p. 95

"The traditional notion of the 'neutrality' of technology can no longer be maintained," Marcuse pointed out in *One-Dimensional Man*. "Technology as such cannot be isolated from the use to which it is put; the technological society is a system of domination which operates already in the concept and construction of techniques." The endless conflicts that Dilbert endures are within the confines of acceptance of that domination. The issues revolve around the finetuning of technique and the calibrating of requisite harshness toward the Dilberts who necessarily must number in the many millions.

The non-decor of Dilbert's office is a fitting metaphor for the arid psychological terrain of the corporate workplace. Parched thirsts have scant hope of being quenched. And the natural world—a tree, a river, and perhaps oneself—is incredibly far from the project that must remain in the foreground.

To ask whether the corporate system might be inherently destructive in human terms is not appropriate. For Dilbert to persist as Dilbert, there can be no context beyond the despised supervisors and familiar cubicles that confine body, mind and spirit.

"As a technological universe," Marcuse wrote, "advanced industrial society is a *political* universe, the latest stage in the realization of a specific historical *project*—namely, the experience, transformation, and organization of nature as the mere stuff of domination."

Other possibilities—personal and social, economic and political, on the job and away from it—become foreclosed by unspoken and routine acceptance. When nature becomes just another raw material, to be experienced and transformed to suit the agendas of corporate bureaucracy, that process "shapes the entire universe of discourse and action, intellectual and material culture." Under marching orders from on-high, technology strides forward—as "culture, politics, and the economy merge into an omnipresent system which swallows up or repulses all alternatives."

We can see, all around us, just how well this functions. The resulting revenues are immense, with huge quantities of various products. We have been the system and it works—irrefutably and, from all indications, inexorably. Or so we're told. We know the drill in our sleep.

Marcuse may have seemed alarmist back in the mid-1960s, but these days his words sound chillingly matter-of-fact in a country where the handshakes of a Clinton and a Gingrich are ongoing: "The productivity and growth potential of this system stabilize the society and contain technical progress within the framework of domination. Technological rationality has become political rationality."

Like Marcuse, cartoonist/essayist Scott Adams has noticed that rampant corporate capitalism involves domination. But while Marcuse sees it as destructive of human potential, Adams posits it as management in need of some fixing.

After escaping a phone-company cubicle, Scott Adams has banked millions, and he's on contract for millions more. He resembles a lobster who has crawled out of the restaurant tank and now sits at the table, napkin in lap, satirizing the spectacle of creatures climbing all over one another.

Zeal to maximize profits has always been vulnerable to charges of deficiency in the soul department. But we live in a very inventive era. Lately, an informal theology has gained media momentum: the divine quest for material wealth.

A decade ago, Leslie Savan dubbed it "secular fiscalism"—"capitalism as an expression of inner spiritual growth." She noted in 1986: "MasterCard's slogan,

Master the Possibilities, is apparently est-inspired. Merrill Lynch's new *Your World Should Know No Boundaries* campaign takes us to God's country..." In 1993, referring to such by-then-common commercials as "spiritual ads," Savan observed that they "help us to simultaneously see our shallow, materialistic ways *and* exorcise them: We can consume the evil of excess by making every purchase into a prayer."

And yet, Savan asks, "don't these ads clang with the contradiction between the abundant material life that commercial culture pushes and the more mystical injunction to shed that abundance in order to focus on what really matters? The contradiction is readily resolved by the ads' *passive* spirituality—be impressed by killer sunsets, feel awe from celestial music—which works right into a consumer kind of spirituality."

In parallel fashion, Scott Adams has a brand of neo-spirituality that works neatly into his impressive—and ongoing—acquisitive frenzy, which he holds out as an inspirational tale for readers.

When Adams gets totally serious in the last chapter of *The Dilbert Future*, he does so with an earnest essay about the marvels of willpower. "I'm turning the humor mode off for this chapter," he writes at the outset.

"Despite the fact that the future will be filled with an ever-growing number of idiots, I remain optimistic," Adams begins. "This chapter will explain why I feel immune from their influence and why you might, too."

While the Adams view of reality has its quirks, it is not particularly idiosyncratic. The bedrock belief system that Adams spells out is widespread among corporate achievers.

Adams is an exemplary believer in what Savan foresaw as "secular fiscalism"—viewing "capitalism as an expression of inner spiritual growth." In his final chapter of *The Dilbert Future*, Adams wanders through twenty pages of musings about physics, time, gravity and psychic phenomena before getting to the final and most crucial section, headed "Affirmations."

Many years ago, Adams heard about a process of affirmations—which he describes as "visualizing what you want and writing it down fifteen times in a row, once a day, until you obtain the thing you visualized." He tried it and got very positive results. "So I picked another goal—to get rich in the stock market," he recalls. "I wrote my affirmation down every day and waited for an inspiration. One day it happened. At about 4:00 A.M., my eyes snapped open, I awoke from a sound sleep, sat bolt upright in bed, and discovered the words 'buy Chrysler' repeating in my head."

Although that bit of inspiration was very much against the conventional wisdom, in retrospect it was brilliant: "That year, Chrysler was arguably the best stock you could have owned."

For Adams, this is the modern secular equivalent of a religious parable. And an epiphany.

He ran another test of affirmations, which got him to buy a software stock that quickly went through the ceiling. "Clearly, this affirmation technique worked." He used it successfully to get into the M.B.A. program at the University of California at Berkeley.

The rest is entrepreneurial history: "I used the affirmations again many times, each time with unlikely success. So much so that by 1988, when I decided I wanted to become a famous syndicated cartoonist, it actually felt like a modest goal." Later on, "I wasn't satisfied that *Dilbert* allowed me to make a comfortable living. I turned my affirmations toward making it the most successful comic on the planet."

Now that an affirmation technique has worked for Scott Adams, he has opted to parade it in front of millions of readers as the ultimately serious punchline of his book, projecting his experience into universality: "In a world with infinite universes, there are infinite chances to get what you want, as well as infinite chances not to. If affirmations help you steer, maybe your odds are a matter of your control."

The notion of a meritocracy has always been a good rationale for extreme inequities. But it can be a hard sell for explaining why so many millions of people are stuck in cubicle jobs—let alone why a baby born into poverty in the South Bronx or South-Central Los Angeles, or Guatemala or Angola, faces such slim chances of healthy survival.

Now, the creator of *Dilbert* has articulated a better rationale: *"Maybe your odds are a matter of your control."*

Inadvertently, Scott Adams has written the ultimate satire of a corporate mentality—in all seriousness.

ACKNOWLEDGEMENTS

I'd like to mention the superb work of people at Common Courage Press—with special thanks for help on this book from Greg Bates, Liz Keith and Tara Townsend.

My sister Helen Solomon, who is quite familiar with cubicles, provided research and insights that were very important to making this book possible.

Bob Harris went out of his way to contribute his astute writing. Dan Perkins ("Tom Tomorrow") and Matt Wuerker, two of the finest political cartoonists in the United States, supplied a wealth of ideas. Tom Frank responded quickly to my call and sent along a number of relevant articles from *The Baffler*, the excellent magazine he edits. Laura Gross, as always, provided valuable advice and assistance as literary agent.

Jeff Cohen, Cheryl Higgins, Michael Hudson, Dan Levy, Robert McChesney and Steve Rhodes offered helpful suggestions about the manuscript. The book's shortcomings, while entirely my doing, are far less severe because of their help.

Indirect but very real inspiration for *The Trouble With Dilbert* came from Ariel Dorfman and Armand Mattelart via their 1971 book *How to Read Donald Duck*, originally published in Chile. *Para Leer al Pato Donald* has survived the book-burners. A quarter of a century later, the Popular Unity remains in many hearts.

To Cheryl Higgins, I owe ineffable thanks.

ABOUT THE AUTHOR

Norman Solomon writes a nationally syndicated column, "Media Beat," distributed to daily newspapers by Creators Syndicate and to weeklies by AlterNet. He is co-author (with Jeff Cohen) of three collections of columns—*Adventures in Medialand: Behind the News, Beyond the Pundits, Through the Media Looking Glass: Decoding Bias and Blather in the News* and *Wizards of Media Oz: Behind the Curtain of Mainstream News*. His book *False Hope: The Politics of Illusion in the Clinton Era* was published in 1994. He is the author of *The Power of Babble* and co-author (with Martin A. Lee) of *Unreliable Sources: A Guide to Detecting Bias in News Media*. His commentary articles have appeared in the *New York Times, Washington Post, Los Angeles Times, Miami Herald, USA Today, International Herald Tribune* and many other newspapers. He has been a guest on C-SPAN, CNN's *Crossfire* and NPR's *Talk of the Nation*. Solomon is executive director of the Institute for Public Accuracy, a nationwide consortium of public-policy experts scrutinizing media releases from major think tanks. Solomon lives in the San Francisco area with his wife, Cheryl Higgins. He can be reached c/o the publisher or via e-mail at <mediabeat@igc.org>.